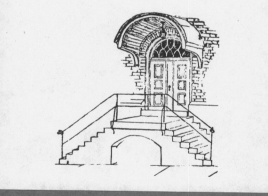

Faulkner's Place

Faulkner's Place

MICHAEL MILLGATE

The University of Georgia Press ATHENS AND LONDON

The paper   © 1997 by the University of Georgia Press

in this   Athens, Georgia 30602

book   All rights reserved

meets the   Set in Monotype Walbaum by G&S Typesetters, Inc.

guidelines   Printed and bound by Braun-Brumfield, Inc.

for   Printed in the United States of America

permanence   01   00   99   98   97   C   5   4   3   2   1

and   Library of Congress Cataloging in Publication Data

durability   Millgate, Michael.

of the   Faulkner's place / by Michael Millgate.

Committee on   p.   cm.

Production   Includes bibliographical references and index.

Guidelines   ISBN 0-8203-1937-6 (alk. paper)

for   1. Faulkner, William, 1897–1962—Criticism and

Book   interpretation.   I. Title.

Longevity   PS3511.A86Z8945   1997

of the   813′.52—dc21   97-15109

Council on   British Library Cataloging in Publication Data available

Library   Photograph on title spread "Building Graphic #1,"

Resources.   © 1996 Marie C. Daum.

To Derry and Jeanne Jeffares

CONTENTS

PREFACE

Seven of the eight essays gathered in this volume were originally written for oral delivery on specific occasions. The eighth, "Faulkner's Masters," was also "occasional" in the sense that it was an invited contribution to a published symposium dedicated to the memory of Richard P. Adams. Six of the essays date from the years 1977 to 1984, the earliest of them, "Faulkner and History," incorporating in this revised version a few paragraphs from a still earlier paper of 1971; only two, "Undue Process" and "Unreal Estate," were written within the last ten years. The volume's contents are thus of their moment in a double sense, conditioned consciously by their anticipated audiences—four of them were presented at the Faulkner conferences held each summer at the University of Mississippi—and, less consciously, by their moments in time.

Those times and their assumptions have of course been left far behind by the rapid and tumultuous advances of Theory. I nevertheless find justification for reviving such essays and such arguments in the year of Faulkner's centenary in the belief that ideas and perceptions grounded in a wide acquaintance with his life, work, and times are unlikely ever to be entirely outdated. My aim and ambition, as I have insisted in the forewords to successive reissues of *The Achievement of William Faulkner,* has always been "to bring scholarship directly to bear upon the processes of criticism, to see the entire range of Faulkner's work within the richest available context of biographical and textual information." That was as true of these relatively informal presentations as of anything else I have written, and in revisiting them I have found reassuringly little that I would now unsay or that subsequent scholarship has clearly invalidated. I have therefore left their arguments essentially unchanged and of their moment, and while it is certainly true that the questions they then asked and the issues they then raised are not those typically addressed by contemporary criticism, the questions remain for the most part unanswered, the issues unresolved, and I must hope and trust that their restatement will help to ensure their continued presence somewhere on the long-term Faulknerian agenda.

By no means all of my previously published Faulkner essays are included here, but I believe that those selected are sufficiently similar in manner and material—perhaps even in a certain lightness of touch—to form a reasonably coherent sequence. In revising them for republication I have felt obliged to omit remarks too narrowly directed at particular audiences, to remove or modify repetitions of quotations and ideas as between one paper and another, and to rephrase passages that seemed to be in need of minor stylistic refurbishment. In incorporating paragraphs from another paper into "Faulkner and History" it also became necessary to delete a portion of the latter. But I have tried throughout to sustain the pervasive sense of a speaking voice, and I have certainly retained most of the autobiographical allusions, digressive asides, and speculative excursions that would normally be excluded from formal academic discourse.

Before attempting to "place" Faulkner in any of the multiple senses made available by my title I should perhaps try to identify my own perspective, my particular point of vantage or disadvantage. A personal anecdote may be helpful: though it has become a little worn through overuse, I may in a volume of this kind be allowed one final invocation. When in the early 1960s I first visited the Faulkner papers at the University of Virginia I encountered on the threshold a distinguished Faulkner collector who looked at me hard and declared: "The trouble with most people who write about Faulkner is that they're Yankees and know nothing about the South." He paused, then added: "You're an Englishman." The statement, unchallengeable in itself, clearly implied a question potentially damaging to my critical and scholarly pretensions. Of course, there were responses I might have made. I could have recalled Faulkner's own aspirations to universality. I could have insisted, as I have often insisted since, that all one really needed to know about Faulkner's region could be found—indeed, could only be found—in Faulkner's books. I could have pleaded Faulkner's personal anglophilia, grounded though it admittedly was in a very limited acquaintance with England and the English. I could even have mentioned that I had spent time in the South, including Oxford itself, some years earlier. Alas, in my eagerness to gain access to his collection I said none of these things but merely shuffled my feet and tugged a figurative forelock.

I nonetheless recognized, and have continued to recognize, that from a southern standpoint the question was, and is, reasonable enough, and when speaking about Faulkner in the South and especially in Mississippi I have sometimes felt a twinge of residual doubt as to the propriety of my addressing such a subject in such a location. It helps to be in the power position on such occasions, armed with a microphone and occupying the higher ground, and since becoming a Canadian I have typically sought to ingratiate myself by invoking my compatriot Shreve McCannon, the surgeon from Edmonton, still practicing there, if the final sentence of *Absalom, Absalom!* is to be believed, but disappointingly not interviewed by any of the Faulkner biographers. Needless to say, I have never discounted the importance of visiting the South, especially Faulkner's personal "place" and places, and I have profited enormously from the Faulkner work and talk ("the best of talking") of such southern scholars as Cleanth Brooks, Thomas L. McHaney, James B. Meriwether, and Noel Polk. At the same time, the distinguished record of French Faulkner scholarship encourages me in the personally sustaining belief that distance is not inevitably a disqualification and that the value and even necessity of an outside view may lie precisely in its independence of local pieties and battles long ago.

In choosing a title susceptible of various readings I am not so much claiming an illusory unity for this volume as pointing toward some of its recurrent concerns. It is obvious enough, for example, that Faulkner's "genius" is on several occasions openly acknowledged and assumed to be his personal possession, and even though his popular and even critical reputation has declined somewhat since the late 1970s—largely as a consequence of his recession in time and his perceived (though generally misunderstood) attitudes toward women, blacks, and native people— I remain profoundly (Faulkner might have said "passionately") convinced that no attentive reader of his best work could doubt its permanent and indeed superlative importance. Not even academic prudence can in any case deter me from committing the unfashionable act of "placing" Faulkner very high indeed among American writers, among novelists writing in English, even among the novelists of the world. The frequent invocation, in "Faulkner's Masters" and elsewhere, of the names of Balzac, Melville, Hardy, Joyce, and other major figures in the history of the novel further emphasizes not just Faulkner's achieved position within that history but the deliberateness with which he sought such distinction by matching himself against admired predecessors and pursuing, in novel after novel, the resolution of fresh technical problems—what Henry James called "beautiful difficulties."

The persistence, energy, and audacity of that pursuit in constant interplay with the sometimes contradictory demands of economic necessity primarily determined the successive stages of Faulkner's career. But the three essays—"The Shape of a Career," "A Cosmos of My Own," and "Faulkner's First Trilogy"—

that speak to my personal fascination with the densely crowded sequences of that career are also concerned, to differing degrees, with the creative significance of geographical "place" as registered in Faulkner's self-consciously regional stance and in the creation and elaboration of his fictional but specifically Mississippian county of Yoknapatawpha. A fourth essay, "The Two Voices," briefly considers Faulkner's sense of himself as a southerner and the implications of his writing about his "own" rural place and people for a potentially hostile, not to say prurient, audience in the cities of the North. Thomas Hardy, the regionalist predecessor discussed alongside Faulkner in "Unreal Estate," has sometimes been criticized for trying always to keep one foot in the door of London even while the other remained firmly planted on the soil of Dorset. But, tricky as such a maneuver might seem, it is at least equalled in complexity by the consequences of Faulkner's attempt to combine his immensely productive literary career with a secondary (if often more profitable) career as a Hollywood screenwriter and with the ownership and restoration of a pre–Civil War house, the subsequent purchase and management of a small farm, the riding and jumping of horses, and, especially in his later years, the pose of being just a simple farmer rather than a man of letters.

Faulkner was from the first a man of poses. They sustained his privacy and self-confidence even as they asserted his artistic integrity and ambition. I first heard from the New Orleans philosopher James K. Feibleman the now well-known story of Faulkner as a little-regarded young man sitting silently drinking among the *Double-Dealer* crowd in New Orleans until the somewhat pretentious literary conversation got around to Shakespeare and to *Hamlet*, at which Faulkner suddenly burst out, "I could write a book like that if I wanted to." He was of course promptly, and properly, laughed down, but as Feibleman observed, he was the only member of that group subsequently to be heard from. The anecdote, embellished or not, has the right note of Faulknerian ambition and arrogance, of the man who could later declare that an artist must be prepared to rob his own mother if need be and add, as if offering sufficient justification, that the "Ode on a Grecian Urn" was worth any number of old ladies. Unfounded though the implicit accusation against Keats may be, there's no doubt that Faulkner himself felt, as an artist, not only ruthless, dedicated, and driven but, so driven, almost unstoppable, well capable of challenging even Shakespeare if need be. And I like to think that, years later, it gave him a certain wry pleasure to change the title of one of his most richly written novels from *The Peasants* to *The Hamlet.*

That revised title, as I suggest in "Unreal Estate," immediately associated the novel with Gray's *Elegy Written in a Country Churchyard* and with the standard conventions and traditions of pastoral literature. But the world of *The Hamlet* is far from serene—Ike's Arcadia, as Lewis Simpson pointed out, exists only in the eye of its specifically idiotic beholder—and its more extravagant, not to say outrageous, elements give some substance to the suspicion that Faulkner's second thought may also have been prompted by memories of the elaborate pastoral artifice of Le Hameau, Marie Antoinette's *ferme ornée* at Versailles, which he visited in 1925. The echo, deliberate or accidental, serves in any case to suggest that in considering the role of place in Faulkner's life and work it is wise not to think of him as simply surrendering to the circumstances of his birth and upbringing. That he was profoundly and inescapably a southerner there can of course be no doubt: it conditioned everything that he thought and wrote. But his use of the South—his own particular "given" portion of the South—as the raw material of his fiction was a matter of personal choice, the consequence of a deliberately adopted literary strategy. Yoknapatawpha County did not just happen, or simply accommodate itself to the circumstances of the place in which Faulkner happened to live. Though perhaps conceived in an instant, it was developed and fabricated and populated with care and over time and in response to its inventor's perceived needs— less a geographical, sociological, or even historical expression than a *paysage moralisé.*

ACKNOWLEDGMENTS

The essays included in this volume first appeared, in somewhat different form, in the publications indicated below, and I gratefully acknowledge permissions to reprint.

"Faulkner and History," in *The South and Faulkner's Yoknapatawpha*, edited by Doreen Fowler and Ann J. Abadie (Jackson: University Press of Mississippi, 1977); also segments of " 'The Firmament of Man's History': Faulkner's Treatment of the Past," *Mississippi Quarterly*, vol. 25 (Spring 1972), Supplement. By permission of the University Press of Mississippi and the Center for the Study of Southern Culture.

"William Faulkner: The Shape of a Career," in *New Directions in Faulkner Studies*, edited by Doreen Fowler and Ann J. Abadie (Jackson: University Press of Mississippi, 1984). By permission of the University Press of Mississippi and the Center for the Study of Southern Culture.

" 'A Cosmos of My Own': The Evolution of Yoknapatawpha" and "Faulkner's First Trilogy: *Sartoris, Sanctuary,* and *Requiem for a Nun,*" in *Fifty Years of Yoknapatawpha,* edited by Doreen Fowler and Ann J. Abadie (Jackson: University Press of Mississippi, 1980). By permission of the University Press of Mississippi and the Center for the Study of Southern Culture.

"William Faulkner: The Two Voices," in *Southern Literature in Transition,* edited by Philip Castille and William Osborne (Memphis: Memphis State University Press, 1983).

"Faulkner's Masters," in *Tulane Studies in English* 23 (1978).

"Undue Process: Faulkner and the Law" (originally titled "Undue Process: William Faulkner's *Sanctuary* "), in *Rough Justice: Essays on Crime in Literature,* edited by Martin L. Friedland (Toronto: University of Toronto Press, 1991).

"Unreal Estate: Reflections on Wessex and Yoknapatawpha," in *The Literature of Region and Nation,* edited by R. P. Draper (Basingstoke: Macmillan Press, 1989).

FAULKNER'S BOOKS: A CHRONOLOGY

1924   *The Marble Faun* (verse)

1926   *Soldiers' Pay* (novel)

1927   *Mosquitoes* (novel)

1929   *Sartoris* (novel) (*Flags in the Dust,* 1973)

1929   *The Sound and the Fury* (novel)

1930   *As I Lay Dying* (novel)

1931   *Sanctuary* (novel)

1931   *These 13* (stories)

1932   *Light in August* (novel)

1933   *A Green Bough* (verse)

1934   *Doctor Martino and Other Stories* (stories)

1935   *Pylon* (novel)

1936   *Absalom, Absalom!* (novel)

1938   *The Unvanquished* (novel)

1939   *The Wild Palms* (novel)

1940   *The Hamlet* (novel)

1942   *Go Down, Moses and Other Stories* (novel)

1948   *Intruder in the Dust* (novel)

1949   *Knight's Gambit* (stories)

1950   *Collected Stories* (stories)

1951   *Requiem for a Nun* (novel)

1954   *A Fable* (novel)

1955   *Big Woods* (stories)

1957   *The Town* (novel)

1959   *The Mansion* (novel)

1962   *The Reivers* (novel)

Faulkner's Place

Faulkner and History

A Canadian may perhaps be allowed to begin by saying something about Shreve McCannon, Quentin Compson's plump friend from Edmonton, Alberta. The point about Shreve as he appears in *Absalom, Absalom!* is not just that he was evidently Faulkner's idea of a domesticated foreigner, but that he was a man unconcerned with his history, and it is worth noting that Faulkner had learned enough from his months in Toronto in 1918 to make his Canadian with a Scottish name (more obviously Scottish than Compson) come from the newly settled prairies and not from, say, Nova Scotia, where Scottish traditions are, even now, vividly and visibly alive. "Because it's something my people haven't got," Shreve says to Quentin in the final chapter. "Or if we have got it, it all happened long ago across the water and so now there aint anything to look at every day to remind us of it. We dont live among defeated grandfathers and freed slaves . . . and bullets in the dining room table and such, to be always reminding us to never forget." [1]

Shreve, with his uncluttered historical memory and his youthful romanticism, has been Quentin's ideal and necessary collaborator in the act of narrative reconstruction to which the novel is largely devoted. Now, the narrative task completed, Shreve wants to identify the meaning of the story they have pieced together, to find the moral of the tale, to understand its significance for the South and specifically for Quentin, through whom it has claimed his attention and participation. That he already has a firm grasp of some of the essential elements is clearly shown in his reference to the bullets in the dining room table and the other southern memorabilia that serve as reminders "to never forget."

To remember is one thing, inseparable from our whole sense of who and what we are. But it is quite another thing, as Faulkner well knew, to formalize not forgetting, to freeze forever into a stiff-necked, unwavering backward gaze. So Miss Rosa, implacable in her hatred, forces her obsessions with the long-dead Sutpen upon a Quentin already sufficiently haunted by "stubborn back-looking ghosts," by "sonorous defeated names."[2] So Faulkner, in the semi-autobiographical piece on "Mississippi" he wrote for *Holiday* magazine, speaks of "the women, the indomitable, the undefeated, who never surrendered, refusing to allow the Yankee *minie* balls to be dug out of portico column or mantelpiece or lintel, who seventy years later would get up and walk out of *Gone With the Wind* as soon as Sherman's name was mentioned." Even in his own childhood, a boy such as himself would know "about Vicksburg and Corinth and exactly where his grandfather's regiment had been at First Manassas before he remembered hearing very much about Santa Claus."[3]

This is familiar ground, of course, but worth returning to simply in order to stress the extent to which Faulkner, as he grew up, was subjected to precisely those pressures to "never forget" subsequently dramatized in books such as *Absalom, Absalom!*, *Flags in the Dust* (published in Faulkner's lifetime only in abbreviated form as *Sartoris*), and *The Unvanquished.* Not only is that what one would have suspected—even now the southern preoccupation with the domestic past can strike an outsider as extraordinary—not only is it confirmed by biographical testimony, but it is there plainly enough in Faulkner's own writings: in the correlation, for example, between the opening of *The Unvanquished* and the passage in the "Mississippi" essay that describes "the boy" acting out Vicksburg and Shiloh and the other "old irremediable battles" with a black child of his own age, "the boy because he was white arrogating to himself the right to be the Confederate General—Pemberton or Johnston or Forrest—twice to the black child's once, else, lacking that once in three, the black one would not play at all." [4]

That Faulkner, like so many of his class and generation in the South, felt the backward pull of southern history, there can be no doubt. How he escaped that pull is not so easy to say. Obviously his wanderings and self-dramatizations as an artist in the 1920s had something to do with it, either as cause or effect. Probably World War I had a good deal to do with it, not least as the occasion of his leaving home and meeting first in New Haven and then in Toronto plenty of people like Shreve McCannon with attitudes and assumptions totally different from his own, more than one of whom no doubt demanded, "*Tell about the South. What's it like there. What do they do there. Why do they live there. Why do they live at all,*" more than one of whom no doubt commented: "The South. Jesus. No wonder you folks all outlive yourselves by years and years and years." [5]

Faulkner clearly recognized in the World War a cataclysmic human event that might well take his own life (the careers of pilots on the Western Front were notoriously short) and certainly dwarfed even the Civil War by its sheer scale and horror. That *Absalom, Absalom!,* though written in the mid-1930s, should have been set in 1910 undoubtedly relates to the fact that at that date Faulkner himself, aged thirteen, was still within perfectly credible touching distance of the Civil War. But the 1910 setting date also prevents the novel from falling under the shadow of the later and greater war that Quentin dodged by his suicide but to which Shreve went, straight from Harvard, as (to quote the Genealogy) "Captain, Royal Army Medical Corps, Canadian Expeditionary Forces, France, 1914–1918"[6]—a dramatic acknowledgment of his own previously deprecated roots that Faulkner cannot have intended to remain unnoticed.

By using 1910 as his temporal vantage point in *Absalom, Absalom!* Faulkner also achieved, perhaps deliberately, an interesting approximation to the classic " 'Tis Sixty Years Since" of Sir Walter Scott's subtitle to *Waverley*. Scott comments in his opening chapter on that sixty-year perspective, making the claim that in representing a period neither absorbingly contemporary nor venerably ancient he has been able to emphasize "the characters and passions of the actors;—those passions common to men in all stages of society, and which have alike agitated the human heart, whether it throbbed under the steel corslet of the fifteenth century, the brocaded coat of the eighteenth, or the blue frock and white dimity waistcoat of the present day."[7] There are obvious similarities between this passage and Faulkner's statements, in the Nobel Prize address and elsewhere, about "the old verities and truths of the heart, the old universal truths lacking which any story is ephemeral and doomed."[8] A comparison can also be drawn between the time-scales of *Waverley* and of *Absalom, Absalom!*: *Waverley* centers upon the events of the Jacobite rebellion of 1745, sixty years before 1805, the time-perspective from which the novel is written; the central historical events of *Absalom, Absalom!* occur within a broader but roughly corresponding period of between seventy-five and forty-five years before 1910. As I have pointed out elsewhere,[9] one might make a further link with Thomas Hardy's interest in the Napoleonic period. Scott, Faulkner, and Hardy are all, in important respects, regional novelists, and each is inevitably drawn to the most disturbed and violent period in the recent past of his own region. There is even a similar time-factor: Scott was born twenty-six years after 1745, Faulkner thirty-two years after the end of the Civil War, Hardy thirty-five years after Trafalgar, twenty-five after Waterloo. Clearly, too, the novelist's imagination was in each instance fed and stirred by listening at an early age to stories told by survivors from those exciting times.

Given these suggestive parallels, is it then proper to go further and posit *Absalom, Absalom!* as a historical novel on the pattern made familiar by Scott and seized upon as a model for historical fiction by critics such as Georg Lukács? Is Faulkner centrally concerned to present his characters as the products or embodiments of their historical moment, to make us feel through their words, thoughts, actions, the inescapable pressures of the times in which they lived? Does he seek to reinforce that presentation in terms of specific, concrete images of the physical world his characters inhabit? Rich though it is as a demonstration of the retrospective imagination at work, *Absalom, Absalom!* seems not in fact to be focused on accuracy of historical representation but rather on the act of historical interpretation in and of itself. The versions of the past variously offered in the novel become important less for any specifically historical light they may throw than for the insight they provide into the respective interpreters, and there is finally a sense in which the novel is not so much about the Sutpen legend as about what the narrators, and especially Quentin, make of that legend—and what the legend makes of Quentin.

Faulkner does have his adventure into historical romance in *The Unvanquished,* and in *Requiem for a Nun* he provides historical sketches not only of the founding and development of Jefferson, Mississippi, but also, in effect, of the creation of the world and the subsequent processes of geological and human evolution. He was also undoubtedly aware of the precedents in historical fiction offered by Scott—and, for that matter, by Tolstoy, Stendhal, Thackeray, Hawthorne, and others. But he seems to have decided, I suspect quite deliberately, against the historical novel proper, and it seems reasonable to suggest, looking at the full range of Faulkner's work, that history as the recording and attempted re-creation of specific periods and events did not greatly interest him. It's not simply that he was notoriously casual about dates, names, and locations in his references to the Civil War, and indeed to the First World War, nor that he often spoke with contempt of facts in general: "I dont care much for facts," he wrote to Malcolm Cowley, "am not much interested in them, you cant stand a fact up, you've got to prop it up, and when you move to one side a little and look at it from that angle, it's not thick enough to cast a shadow in that direction." [10] It's rather a matter of his having been altogether less concerned with history as conventionally understood than with a much vaguer, vaster, less manageable entity called the past.

In *Absalom, Absalom!* one can almost speak of a battle for domination over the present being fought out between the past on the one hand and history on the other—between a formless mass of dark, vaguely guilt-ridden memories, rumors, and prejudices, and the deliberate, artistic shaping of a complete, coherent, intelligible narrative. What we watch in the latter part of the novel is the process by which Shreve—self-cast as confessor, psychiatrist, interlocutor, agent provocateur, Doctor Watson, academic collaborator, or what you will—assists Quentin in assessing the raw, undigested information about the past he has received from various sources and in making sense of that information, turning it into narrative. The collaboration is a brilliant quasi-authorial success, reaching its climax at the end of chapter 8 with that magnificently realized, unmediated evocation of how it must have been when Sutpen, in the dying days of the Civil War, called Henry to his tent and told him about the circumstances of Charles Bon's birth. In chapter 9, however, the collaboration breaks down over the question of interpretation. Quentin and Shreve have achieved a moment of apotheosis, brought all their knowledge cumulatively to bear upon a single moment, narrated together the ideal Faulknerian novel. But though they have had the moment they have missed the meaning, and in a mood of *post fabulam tristis* find themselves once more lost and apart. The ghosts that intellect and imagination and narrative art had seemed to control and exorcise now come sweeping back as Quentin confronts at last the memory he has been avoiding throughout, that of his encounter with the spectral, death-in-life figure of Henry Sutpen in the Gothic darkness of the decaying mansion. And as the book ends—despite all Shreve's attempts, well-meant if not especially subtle, to get through to him— Quentin is drawn, gasping for breath, back into the chaotic vortex of the past.

Quentin's final words and thoughts, "*I dont hate it! I dont hate it!,*" [11] are directly echoed in the "Mississippi" essay: "Home again, his native land; he was born of it and his bones will sleep in it; loving it even while hating some of it." [12] But if Quentin's dilemma is in some sense exemplary, it does not follow that we are to regard his fate as typical. Faulkner, unlike so many of his characters, seems *not* to have believed that we necessarily carry our past around with us on our earthly pilgrimage like an unshiftable burden upon our backs, a miasmic doom-laden cloud hanging always an inch or two above our cringing heads. In the very act of escaping from the southern obsession with the past Faulkner seems to have sensed that he could use it creatively as a means of dramatizing his own perception, heightened by exposure to that obsession, that life was and could only be motion, that without movement, change, activity there could be no life but only a form of death. He saw early—there are hints even in *The Marble Faun*, much stronger ones in *Soldiers' Pay*—that while stasis may have its dignity and its powerful moral and aesthetic attractions it has also terrible dangers. He saw too that celebration of the values of the past need not imply rejection of the present, indeed must not involve such rejection if those older values are to retain their vitality and validity.

In the early works these conceptions are neither clearly held nor consistently worked out. In the unpublished story "Rose of Lebanon," probably written in the middle or late 1920s, they are rather extravagantly explored through the figure of Gavin Blount who, in his infatuation with a romanticized past, proposes marriage at the age of forty-three to the eighty-two-year-old woman who had kissed all the one hundred and four men of her husband's newly formed regiment before they rode off to fight at Shiloh. The redoubtable lady responds by throwing a bowl of soup over her suitor, ostensibly by way of demonstrating how she had repelled Yankees. Faulkner showed his own sense of appropriate action by leaving the story unpublished. But Gavin Blount subsequently bequeathed more than his first name to the comprehensively romantic Gavin Stevens and had a more direct heir in the past-bound Gail Hightower of *Light in August.* Like the Quentin Compson of *Absalom, Absalom!* and the Ike McCaslin of *Go Down, Moses*—the recurrence of the situation testifies to the depth and persistence of Faulkner's concern—Hightower in his fixation upon the past is incapable of living fully in the present, with consequences that are disastrous not only for himself but for others.

The past upon which these characters brood may not in itself be evil or even unadmirable. Sutpen and his children had many qualities of strength, endurance, and capacity for action that Quentin himself might have done well to emulate. Ike McCaslin was right to regret the destruction of the wilderness. Faulkner once acknowledged in an interview that there was something fine and brave about the Civil War grandfather with whose galloping figure Hightower has identified himself. The overall movement and pressure of each novel nonetheless work inexorably to enforce what was perhaps Faulkner's single most fundamental belief—that life was motion, that, like it or not, there was no way of retrieving the past, restoring lost environments, winning the irremediable battles—that it was even truer in temporal than in geographical terms that one could not go home again.

If I repeat these perhaps self-evident points, that is chiefly because readers persist in looking for individual characters who appear to speak "for" Faulkner—in searching for neat quotable formulations instead of responding to the total experience of the novels themselves. *The Sound and the Fury* has gained a reputation as the quintessential modernist novel, an outstanding example of "objectivity" in fiction, a work from which the author has rather obtrusively absented himself. (In truth, of course, it was only from *As I Lay Dying* that Faulkner can in any sense be said to have absconded completely; he was only in the process of absconding from *The Sound and the Fury* and seems always to have retained a sense of having failed to follow through the logic of the novel's technique.) I rather doubt Faulkner's ever believing that it was more "objective" for the author to absent himself formally from his work in this manner, but he surely felt that it was somehow truer, more forceful, more "passionate." As he observed at Nagano: "[E]very man has a different idea of what's beautiful. And it's best to take the gesture, the shadow of the branch, and let the mind create the tree."[13] Work not by direct intrusive commentary, not through deliberately planted authorial mouthpieces, but by implication; involve the reader directly in the constructive and imaginative processes; allow the shape and splendor of the tree to emerge at or after the end of the novel, the product of a collaborative experience, different for each individual reader but subtly directed and stimulated by the author throughout—nominally an absentee landlord but keeping in fact the tightest possible hold on all the essential terms of the lease.

Faulkner thoroughly understood all these now much discussed matters and even articulated them, in his deceptively simplistic way. When someone asked him whether *Absalom, Absalom!* didn't offer, in effect, thirteen different ways of looking at the blackbird, Faulkner agreed, adding: "But the truth, I would like to think, comes out, that when the reader has read all these thirteen ways of looking at the blackbird, the reader has his own fourteenth image of that blackbird which I would like to think is the truth."[14] What still seems insufficiently appreciated is that Faulkner works essentially in this manner in all of his fiction, not just in such obviously experimental works as *The Sound and the*

Fury and *As I Lay Dying*. His basic method depends upon each work being read as a whole. Each individual episode, character, chapter has its meaning and function in terms of the whole and must be seen in relation to, in reverberation with, all the other episodes, characters, chapters. His approach is one of indirection, of inexplicitness. His direct addresses to the reader take the form of his successive acts of completing and publishing each of the books in turn. And what he says each time is what he said to Ben Wasson when handing him the completed manuscript of *The Sound and the Fury:* "Read this, Bud. It's a real sonofabitch." [15]

Given such a method, it's clearly unsafe to depend upon the viewpoint or formulations of any single voice, however persuasive, wise, or dominating it may seem. When Gavin Stevens theorizes about Joe Christmas in *Light in August* or Ike McCaslin ruminates upon southern history in *Go Down, Moses*, Faulkner counts upon our perceiving (as in *Absalom, Absalom!*) that they are telling us more about themselves than about their ostensible subjects. Even Ratliff, perhaps the most attractive observer figure in all of Faulkner, is in some degree to be distrusted because he *is* an observer—because as a bachelor, an itinerant, a man of some economic independence, he is too little involved in the kinds of basic human and economic needs that necessarily preoccupy the inhabitants of Frenchman's Bend. Conversely, it is dangerous to close one's ears to any Faulknerian voices. In *The Sound and the Fury,* as Linda Wagner has shown,[16] there is a case to be made even for Jason Compson, and it is one that might gain a sympathetic hearing if he were being tried before a grievance tribunal instead of at the bar of the eternal verities. In *Absalom, Absalom!* Miss Rosa's voice does not in the end dominate, but neither is it wholly suppressed. In *Requiem for a Nun,* where the processes of judgment are specifically invoked in a series of courtroom situations and quasi-judicial hearings, it is essential that we listen to Temple Drake as well as to Gavin Stevens and Nancy Mannigoe.

Requiem for a Nun of course contains what is perhaps the most often quoted statement about the past in all of Faulkner's work—

and probably, because so often read out of context, the most misunderstood. "The past," declares Gavin Stevens, "is never dead. It's not even past." [17] Part of the difficulty with the quotation is that it consists of two statements not necessarily interdependent. That the past is, in a sense, never dead—that it is always sufficiently alive to haunt the present—Faulkner's whole work goes to show. No one was more sensitive to the survival into the present of witnesses to the fact that individual human beings *were* in the past, that they lived, moved, and left permanent records of that life and movement in the form of letters, tombstones, scratches on windowpanes, entries in commissary books—just as the artist, in Faulkner's favorite phrase, seeks through the legacy of his work to write "Kilroy was here" on the walls of the world. (Though that ambition perhaps does not sufficiently allow for the danger, encountered by Joyce Cary's artist Gulley Jimson, that the walls may themselves disappear.) Faulkner is also acutely aware of the processes of human heredity and the succession of the generations. Nowhere, perhaps, is he more perceptively and movingly the historian than in his sensitivity to the provenance of Yoknapatawpha names—to the presence of Grenier behind Grinnup in *Knight's Gambit,* of Bondurant (presumably) behind Bundren in *As I Lay Dying*—or to the survival of racial characteristics: in the "Mississippi" article, for example, he speaks of the Indian features occasionally encountered looking out of a white or black face, of the old pre-Culloden feuding still practiced in the hill country among families with Scottish names.

Faulkner's whole ambition as a novelist, moreover, was the magnificent but impossible one of saying it all in one sentence, between "one cap and one period," of bringing to bear the total experience of the past—all the light rays, as he liked to put it— upon individual moments of human experience. In *Faulkner in the University* he speaks of the poet as finding that "man's history in its mutations, in the instances in which it becomes apparent," becomes "so strong and so urgent that it must be recorded." [18] Faulkner's term "apparent" has obvious affinities with Joyce's term "epiphany" and seems to carry a similar meaning: that there are moments in individual lives of such extraordinary intensity that they become revelatory, eloquent, of fundamental human truths—the spirit becomes flesh, as it were, hence accessible to the artist. But it is also clear that by man's history Faulkner means, here as elsewhere, not just man's past but his present and future also. In another passage in *Faulkner in the University* Faulkner, speaking in 1957, insists that if there were a machine capable of projecting into the future "that machine could isolate and freeze a picture, an image, of what man will be doing in 2057, just as the machine might capture and fix the light rays showing what he was doing in B.C. 28. That is, that's the mystical belief that there is no such thing as *was*. That time *is*, and if there's no such thing as *was*, then there is no such thing as *will be*. That time is not a fixed condition, time is in a way the sum of the combined intelligences of all men who breathe at that moment." [19]

Time is seen here not so much as a sequence but as a continuum, like space, and it appears from other passages, including the narrative prologues of *Requiem for a Nun*, that Faulkner saw human nature itself as a kind of continuum, always essentially the same yet proceeding through successive versions or avatars of itself, each becoming obsolete in its turn and yielding place to a successor. This is not a developmental view—Faulkner does not see mankind as moving toward any far-off divine event, nor does he entertain illusions of human perfectibility. There seems to be little "progress" save in a purely cumulative sense, like the layering of geological strata one upon another. But neither is it a pessimistic view: human nature is seen as perpetually adjusting itself to the needs of its particular moment and consistently displaying those basic capacities for survival—strength and rapacity and cunning as well as love and compassion and sacrifice—on which Faulkner bases his belief that mankind will not only survive but prevail. He is not optimistic about either the morality or the fate of individual human beings, but he has absolute faith in the future of the human race. There may indeed be disasters, as there have been at other periods, but even after a nuclear holocaust the human race would still endure.

Evidently Gavin Stevens—to return to him at last—gets a general endorsement from the rest of Faulkner's writings for his statement that the past is not dead. Logically, too, it might be argued that Faulkner's view of time as a continuum is also supportive of Stevens's assertion that the past isn't even past. But within the context of the novel Stevens isn't speaking in such terms, his assertion rather falling into place as part of an attitude toward the business of actual living that Faulkner seems *not* to endorse. Though *Requiem* remains one of the most enigmatic of Faulkner's works, Noel Polk is surely right to insist[20] that the novel enforces a radical criticism of Stevens's increasingly arid pursuit of an abstract conception of justice and truth, his obsessive concern with the past, and his insensitivity toward the present—toward Temple's suffering over the loss of her child, her courageous attempts to sustain Gowan's self-esteem and keep their marriage afloat, and her genuine concern for Nancy (whom Stevens, her lawyer, seems to have written off long ago). Stevens may believe and live by the presence and even primacy of the past, but Temple is totally absorbed in the difficult and painful business of living from day to day.

Even if *Requiem* is offering, as Faulkner's novels so often do offer, a quasi-dialectical situation in which there is something to be said on both sides (as in the debate between the General and the Corporal in *A Fable* or the argument between Ike and Cass in *Go Down, Moses*), it clearly demands sympathy for Temple in her confrontation with the actualities of the present and the future ("tomorrow, and tomorrow, and tomorrow" are words often on her lips). It also prompts suspicion of a romantic idealism that in Stevens, as in Quentin, Ike, and Hightower, finds its richest soil in an obsession with the past. What the novel seems finally to propose is that it is one thing to recognize that the past is not dead, that mankind is permanently the same, that we all have origins, roots, hereditary characteristics, memories, and guilts, but that it is quite another thing to submit our lives to the control of that past, to insist, as Stevens does, not just upon remembering but upon reminding ourselves and others to never forget.

At the conclusion of Robert Penn Warren's *All the King's Men*, published in 1946, Jack Burden declares: "[S]oon now we shall go out of the house and go into the convulsion of the world, out of history into history and the awful responsibility of Time."[21] Underlying the rhetorical inflation in this passage is an idea roughly approximating to what I take Faulkner to be implicitly recommending in *Requiem* and in *Go Down, Moses*. Asked about *All the King's Men* at Nagano, however, Faulkner declared: "the only thing good in that book, and that was very good, was a story which [Warren] put into the middle of it. I don't know why except he thought it was an awful good story himself, that's probably the reason. But for me, I would have kept that story and thrown the rest of the book away."[22] The "story" in question is obviously the central, ostensibly detachable, Cass Mastern narrative, and Faulkner, far from failing to understand its function within the novel, must clearly have recognized it as a deeply imagined and richly worked moral fable embedded—separate, complete, intact, powerful—in the heart of the novel, enforcing without overt commentary the message the central first-person narrative articulates, rather too self-consciously, on the author's behalf.

As such, the Cass Mastern narrative was essentially of a kind with those fabular embodiments of universal human experiences and truths that Faulkner had often incorporated into works of his own: the story of the bear and the dog in *Go Down, Moses*, the transcendent love story of Ike and the cow in *The Hamlet*, the story of the stolen racehorse in *A Fable*. Literary and classical allusions are often drawn upon—Keats is much invoked in *Go Down, Moses*, Ike's cow becomes a Juno figure—and in *A Fable* Faulkner writes of the groom's devotion to the crippled horse in a kind of rhetorical ecstasy as "the immortal pageant-piece of the tender legend which was the crowning glory of man's own legend beginning when his first paired children lost well the world and from which paired prototypes they still challenged paradise, still paired and still immortal against the chronicle's grimed and bloodstained pages: Adam and Lilith and Paris and Helen and Pyramus and Thisbe and all the other recordless Romeos and their Juliets." The extended sentence concludes: "being immortal, the story, the legend, was not to be owned by any one of the pairs who added to its shining and tragic increment, but only to be used, passed through, by each in their doomed and homeless turn." [23] The groom in *A Fable* may be an unattractive figure (as Ike Snopes had perhaps been in *The Hamlet*), but his story is of a piece with the stories of the world's greatest legendary lovers—is in fact the same story, in which the groom has been called for his brief moment to act, a local roadshow version, so to speak, of a classic, permanently valid, fable of the human capacity for all-surrendering love.

Faulkner's fables thus exist and speak in their own right, as independent fictions, and at the same time powerfully affect the reader's total apprehension of the works in which they are incorporated: in *A Fable*, itself a compendium of fables, the horse-thieves' story is, among many other things, a signal as to how we should read the pervasive background fable of the Crucifixion. Fables are also an essential element in what Faulkner understands by history. As he says, again in *A Fable*, the great classical and traditional legends—"all the celestial zoology of horse and goat and swan and bull"—have been the supreme embodiments and perpetuators of permanent human truths, constituting "the firmament of man's history instead of the mere rubble of his past." [24]

That mere rubble is what seems to impinge upon so many of Faulkner's characters as they look around them at the visible world or peer obsessively and shortsightedly back into their own or their families' immediate backgrounds. The wiser course—for them and, implicitly, for us—would be to live actively in the present in the light of those truths distilled from the entirety of human experience. And the artist's task, as Faulkner perceives it, is to perform that task of distillation, to make permanent in art those moments in the perpetual motion of the world, the unceasing interaction of human lives, in which we can suddenly catch in the particular a glimpse of the universal. This, presumably, is what Faulkner means when he speaks of those epiphanal instants when human history becomes "apparent," using that term much as Whitman does in "Crossing Brooklyn Ferry" when he praises "appearances" as those "dumb, beautiful ministers" who make possible some apprehension of the eternal.

The past, it seems, interested Faulkner not so much for its own sake as because it provided a text for the study of humankind. Or rather an inexhaustible series of texts. When Simon Claxton, one of his last interviewers, and one of the few to catch him at Rowanoak, asked what advice he would give to a prospective writer, Faulkner replied: "Read a lot, and of everything—fiction, biography, history, law. I read all the law and medical books of my father and grandfather. Because they were dealing with men, with Man in his human dilemma." A moment or two later Faulkner responded with characteristic simplicity, clarity, and concision to a question as to whether in order to understand the South it was necessary to know its history: "Only in so far as history is the work of men and we should thus learn all we can from it. It always has its uses. I *wanted* to learn about the South— that's why I read history. But we aren't specifically concerned with it, though it is always round us. Mankind was in the past, and is in the present and will be in the future." [25]

William Faulkner: The Shape of a Career

Dictionaries customarily define "career" as "a person's course or progress through life" or as "a profession affording opportunities for advancement"—as once upon a time it used to be possible to speak of "an academic career." But that usage of the word apparently doesn't date back beyond the beginning of the nineteenth century. Earlier, and still available, meanings of the word include "a race-course," "a short gallop at full speed," "a (swift) running course, as of the sun or a star through the heavens," and more abstractly, "full speed, impetus." (I quote from the *Shorter Oxford English Dictionary,* but Webster reads almost exactly the same.) Accustomed as we are to think of an author's career as something finished and finite, as the posthumous listing of completed works, it does no harm to be reminded that the bibliographical record is simply the frozen retrospect—collected and re-collected in academic tranquillity—of what was created by the author in and through profound emotion and excitement. At the time when it was in progress that career may indeed have been a gallop at full speed, its impetus little short of headlong.

That is spectacularly true, I suggest, of William Faulkner's career, particularly during the extraordinarily productive period that began in 1929 with the writing and publication of *The Sound and the Fury*, and I want to raise here the question of whether he was then directing his energies with some deliberateness toward preconceived goals or simply giving those energies their head—running not so much a race along a marked course as hunting after an always elusive experience of final and absolute creative achievement, taking each unanticipated hedge as it came and only at a later stage looking back over the route he had taken, the career through which he had, so to speak, careered. The short story "Carcassonne," often read as an early statement of creative aspiration, points strongly in the latter direction: "*And me on a buckskin pony with eyes like blue electricity and a mane like tangled fire, galloping up the hill and right off into the high heaven of the world.*" [1] But the statements Faulkner made in later life are often quite different in their emphases: after writing *Soldiers' Pay*, he told Jean Stein in 1955, he found out "that not only each book had to have a design but the whole output or sum of an artist's work had to have a design." [2]

Gary Lee Stonum would have us think of a literary career as a sequence of prospective and retrospective decisions more or less consciously taken, of texts played off against one another in almost dialectical fashion, each book responding in some degree to its predecessor and predetermining in some degree the shape of its successor. [3] He offers analogies that serve to suggest that such processes occur in conformity with general laws and may therefore be expected to manifest themselves within any career of reasonable length. But attractive and suggestive as this approach may be in many ways, the multiplicity of Faulkner's work, the sheer density of his career, renders its application to his case peculiarly resistant to effective demonstration. And by declining to consider the role of Yoknapatawpha County or indeed of any overall directive principles that might conceivably be operative, Stonum effectively sidesteps the question of whether or not there was any larger framework within which the interplay between one book and another was being conducted—any larger strategies to which such tactical maneuverings could be seen to relate.

For those of us who do not plan our work on a long-term basis, who gaze around us in pleased surprise at the discovery that we have finished something and might yet live to tackle something else, it is not hard to think of a career as a series of events either unrelated one to another or as related merely through alternation—in the sense that having done one sort of thing one might well do a different sort of thing, for variety's or self-education's or promotion's or simply occupation's sake. Contrapuntal without integration. Yet nothing is more obvious than that historians and scholars are perpetually embarking upon Declines and Falls and Oxford English Dictionaries and editions of Rousseau and Boswell that they have no right to expect that they will see the end of. And writers such as Balzac, Zola, and Proust have boldly undertaken sequences of novels whose hoped-for completion must lie years and even decades in the future. It is true that the French seem best capable of handling such Napoleonic ambitions in Napoleonic fashion, but it would clearly not have been unprecedented for Faulkner to have projected a patterned series of novels early in his career and devoted himself thereafter to its completion.

There is ground to be cleared, however, before we can address ourselves at all usefully to the question of how far Faulkner can be said to have set himself such a goal. And some ground that will perhaps never be satisfactorily cleared. When we speak, loosely, of an author's career, we tend to do so in terms of publication dates. Faulkner's career, we say, began with *The Marble Faun* (1924) and ended with *The Reivers* (1962). But even those scholars who have explored that career in detail can rarely have incorporated into their sense of its progression any adequate recognition of the short stories, poems, essays, and film scripts composed during the intervals between the publication dates of novels. By hiving such items off into separate categories we are implicitly acknowledging our own limitations, groping for a way of maintaining some sort of intellectual grasp of what must for Faulkner have been a teeming reality of every day.

Even a bibliographical listing that included in a single sequence the publication dates of all of Faulkner's works, large and small, would still be sadly inadequate as a reflection of that reality. For it would be a record of public events only, events all too often conditioned by accidents of history and biography, by the exigencies of the marketplace, the quirks of printers, and the whims of editors. It would tell us very little about the actual composition and revision of particular works—about the origins of *The Sound and the Fury*, for example, the carving of *Sartoris* out of *Flags in the Dust*, or the long gestation of *A Fable*—and it would provide no clear sense of how any particular work was related, in point of time, to this or that other work. Moreover, Faulkner's tendency to write in holograph and on the typewriter almost in tandem—often typing up his manuscripts as he went along instead of waiting until any single form of the work had been completed in its entirety—renders it extremely difficult, sometimes impossible, to make statements about the detailed histories of particular texts that are at once reasonably simple and reasonably accurate. And since he generally destroyed his rejected drafts, those manuscripts and typescripts that do survive may represent only a tiny proportion of those that once existed.

Who is to tell, now, how far the published *Requiem for a Nun* of 1951 harks back to the abortive *Requiem* that was projected and started in 1933? Of what kind and what length were the "three manuscripts" of which Faulkner said in 1957 that they "never did quite please me and I burned them up"?[4] (All we know about them is that they did not refer to the period between 1870 and 1912–14.)[5] Would *The Wild Palms* have been differently perceived, at the time of its publication and since, if Faulkner had been permitted to retain his preferred title, "If I Forget Thee, Jerusalem,"[6] or if Random House had accepted in 1946 his suggestion that the "Wild Palms" segment be included, rather than *As I Lay Dying*, with the Modern Library reprint of *The Sound and the Fury* that for so long served as a standard college text?[7] What other novels and stories would we have had if Faulkner had not felt obliged to work in Hollywood for extended periods? Was the fiction he did complete significantly affected by his Hollywood experience? How long a gap would there have been between *Go Down, Moses* (published in 1942) and *Intruder in the Dust* (published in 1948, but projected in 1940) if World War II had not occurred? Had there been no war, how would *The Mansion* have been narratively worked out? Would *A Fable* have been written at all?

I do not for a moment suggest that Faulkner was the only novelist whose career was affected by external events—although it could certainly be said that some other novelists have had greater control over their circumstances and even (though this is more rare) over their publishers: Sir Frederick Macmillan, for example, always took the position that he could not afford to disoblige an author of Thomas Hardy's standing—for which read, at least in part, of Thomas Hardy's profitability. My point is simply that Faulkner's career may have very imperfectly embodied his own ambitions for it and that, in any case, the standard forms of recording such a career give us very little impression of its internal realities. A comprehensive date book—a *Faulkner Log*, a *Days and Hours of William Faulkner*—might prove a somewhat more sensitive indicator of what Faulkner was writing when, but I suspect that what is really needed (and what I cannot, alas, offer to provide) is some elaborate graphic representation of the sequence and overlapping of his multifarious undertakings. Done in different colored inks, perhaps.

However difficult, even impossible, it may be to comprehend Faulkner's career in its full complexity, it still seems appropriate and indeed necessary to ask questions about his sense, early and late, of that career's direction. Can one tell, despite the inadequacy of the evidence, whether there was a consistent design running through that intricate mesh of creative threads? Did he carry with him a conceptual map of what the completed *oeuvre* should ideally look like? Was he able—would he have been able—to look back after the publication of *The Reivers* and cry "It is good!" Or even, since he always had a secure sense of his own creative standing, "It is God!" To what extent, specifically, had he realized at the end of his career the promise of that visionary moment when, back in the mid-1920s, he "thought of the whole story at once like a bolt of lightning lights up a landscape and you see everything"?[8]

The difficulty here, of course, is that we do not know what exactly it was that Faulkner saw. The "whole story" of what? And what did he mean by "story"? Not, I think, the plots of *Light in August, Absalom, Absalom!, The Wild Palms,* or even *The Sound and the Fury.* He made the statement at the University of Virginia while responding to a question about the origins of *The Hamlet,* and we need not doubt, I think, that by the mid-1920s he foresaw "Father Abraham" and the broad pattern of events that might potentially fall into place around the career of Flem Snopes—as that career is summarized, for example, in the pages of *Sartoris.*[9] He presumably saw, too, how the central idea of the Snopeses' progress, their spreading like "mold over cheese,"[10] could provide the vehicle for an expansive sociohistorical presentation of an imaginary world that would recognizably correspond to the familiar actualities of his native region, whatever the distorting effects of symbolism, fable, fantasy, satire, and humor. (Remember that his vision was of a landscape seen not by the light of day but in the altogether less normative illumination of a nighttime lightning flash.) Doubtless he further recognized, at least in general terms, how the kinds of stories he had been hearing all his life could find a hospitable location within the loose narrative structures by which that world would be constituted, given realization and substance.

What, indeed, he seems chiefly to have glimpsed and grasped in that seminal moment was not so much a specific "story" as the possibility and promise of narrative acts on a scale commensurate with the reach of his literary ambition. He saw (even if he could not yet name) Yoknapatawpha County both as imposing coherence on a mass of perceived but as yet unabsorbed material and as giving access to an infinite range of tales and tellers. The regional definition validated the exploitation of the tale-telling convention, and that convention offered a basic situation of fictional narrator and dramatically present fictional narratee that could be exploited in many different ways and to many different ends—above all as a means of bringing the experience and emotions of the past immediately to bear upon the consciousness of the present. (Such situations remained available, of course, throughout his career, up to and including the "Grandfather said" of *The Reivers*.) [11] Meanwhile the fundamental conception of a region developing and changing through time made it possible to think of narrative material from different social strata and from different dates as being at least minimally interconnected through the direct experience of socially mobile central characters (salesmen, lawyers, doctors, children) or through structural devices of contrastive juxtaposition.

Seized with such possibilities, Faulkner appears to have launched upon several different projects almost simultaneously: upon what eventually became the Snopes trilogy, upon a Sartoris/Benbow narrative that achieved at least fragmentary publication as *Sartoris* and *Sanctuary* (perhaps also as parts of *The Unvanquished*), and upon a series of regional short stories for which Quentin Compson was at one stage to have been the central narrator—a project that perhaps found partial realization in *These 13* and *Go Down, Moses*. In each instance the structural control was loose, what we have become accustomed to call episodic, and the narrative was built up in blocks that were related one to another by contrast, by regional affinity, and by the interweaving paths of the pivotal characters—Bayard Sartoris and Horace Benbow, for instance—who were themselves linked by contrast and by locality even though they might rarely or never meet. If it is easy, and familiar, enough to think of *Sartoris* in such terms—easier still when it is read in that earlier, fuller version approximately available to us as *Flags in the Dust*—it is not difficult, either, to see those same terms as broadly applicable to *Sanctuary, The Hamlet, The Town,* and *The Mansion,* or even to *Go Down, Moses.*

I profoundly suspect—criticism believes before scholarship demonstrates, or even, in this instance, without scholarly demonstration—that the origins of *Sanctuary* date from before the conception and completion of *The Sound and the Fury,* and that it emerged from the inchoate mass of partly written, partly conceptualized, narrative that also included not just "Father Abraham" and other Snopes episodes but the Sartoris material of *Flags in the Dust, The Unvanquished,* and such war stories as "All the Dead Pilots," "Ad Astra," and "With Caution and Dispatch." Horace Benbow himself may well have been central to much of this material, partly as a first sketch for the kind of sensitive, neurotic character (fit vehicle for streams or at least trickles of Joycean consciousness) whom Faulkner's evolving genius was shortly to transform into the Quentin Compson of *The Sound and the Fury,* more substantially as a naively crusading lawyer moving through different strata of the regional society, allied to the established power structure yet liable through choice or chance to become involved with the likes of Popeye, Miss Reba, and Nancy Mannigoe. This, of course, was the role Faulkner was later to assign to Gavin Stevens, and since in taking over much of Horace's background and personality Stevens seems also to have taken over some of the narratives with which he was associated, it seems feasible to think not just of *The Town* and *The Mansion* but also of *Knight's Gambit* and even *Intruder in the Dust* as ultimately referable back to Faulkner's original mid-1920s conception.

By the time they eventually appeared, even such works as *The Town* and *The Mansion* had of course grown to be very different from Faulkner's first idea of them. Little survives in *The Mansion* as published of the outline Faulkner supplied to Robert

Haas of Random House in December 1938, when *The Hamlet* was still called "The Peasants" while *The Town* was projected as "Rus in Urbe" and *The Mansion* itself as "Ilium Falling."[12] By the time he had completed *The Hamlet* the following fall, however, Faulkner had settled on the final titles of all three novels and on a plan for the defeat of Senator Clarence Snopes.[13] That plan, or part of it, was in the event used to get Montgomery Ward Snopes into jail in *The Town*, the actual disposal of the Senator in *The Mansion* occurring within the context of historical events that Faulkner in 1939 could scarcely have foreseen, and of tall tale contrivances that he might have done well to forget. As he and the world grew older, as the body of his work itself grew larger, generating its own patterns and its own dynamic, Yoknapatawpha could scarcely remain unaffected and unchanged—as Faulkner himself acknowledged in that author's note to *The Mansion* in which he ingeniously and only a trifle disingenuously justified—on grounds of long cohabitation with his characters—the narrative discrepancies between that book and its predecessors in the trilogy.

My speculation, then, is that *Soldiers' Pay* and *Mosquitoes* predated Faulkner's moment of vision (they may, of course, have contributed, positively or negatively, to its occurrence) but that several subsequent works may have derived quite directly from it: *Sartoris (Flags in the Dust)*, *Sanctuary*, *These 13*, *The Unvanquished*, *The Hamlet*, *Go Down, Moses*, *The Town*, and *The Mansion*. Three other books, *Intruder in the Dust*, *Knight's Gambit*, and *The Reivers*, seem to fall into a secondary category as having been generated by texts that themselves figure in the primary list I have just offered. Perhaps one could add *Big Woods* and *Collected Stories* as well. For each of these texts I believe that one could draw a fairly convincing stemma or family tree demonstrative of its direct or indirect descent from that moment when Faulkner saw "the whole story at once."

They are, by and large, the works in which the elaboration of Yoknapatawpha County for its own sake—its geography, economy, history, demography, class-structure—is most specifically, centrally, and extensively conducted. As I suggested earlier, they also display a considerable degree of technical consistency, carrying through to the end of Faulkner's career those narrative methods and structures that had first been adopted in *Flags in the Dust.* That is not, of course, to say that they are necessarily lacking in technical finish or even in technical innovation, but it is, I think, to imply that they represent, collectively, a relatively conventional strand within Faulkner's achievement as a whole, *textes de plaisir* rather than *textes de jouissance.* Dare I also venture the suggestion that they tend to embody a generally conservative set of moral positions? They certainly include the texts upon which Noel Polk principally depended in his 1979 paper on "Faulkner and Respectability." [14]

It is noticeable that most of the books on the list fall within the latter part of Faulkner's career. It has always been clear that as the years passed he became increasingly concerned to elaborate on paper his matured conception of his fictional world, to fill it out in both historical and social terms, to give it greater solidity, to strengthen (so to speak) its defenses. The Compson "Appendix," the cooperation with Malcolm Cowley in the preparation of *The Portable Faulkner,* the prologues to *Requiem for a Nun*—these were only the most obvious signals of an intention everywhere apparent. At the same time it seems necessary to entertain the possibility that Faulkner may from time to time (during his difficulties with *A Fable,* for example) have turned back to long-familiar and long-pondered conceptions, even to already existing manuscripts, with a certain sense of relief—knowing that they could be depended upon to be creatively manageable, and to provide, in most instances, congenial contexts for the indirect expression of his own middle-aged opinions.

It was certainly not so in those years between *The Sound and the Fury* and *The Wild Palms* when Faulkner's career was indeed a gallop at full speed. If in writing *Flags in the Dust* and publishing *Sartoris* he established his claim to a region and a society, it was in writing *The Sound and the Fury* that he discovered the challenge and excitement, the all-absorbing passion, of the struggle with form. With *The Sound and the Fury* another Faulknerian voice—that of the modernist, radical experimentalist, and untrammelled moralist—for the first time makes itself clearly audible, and for roughly a dozen years following the completion of *Flags in the Dust* it is possible to perceive the outline of a fairly regular alternation between what might be called aboriginal, essentially conservative, works on the one hand and more opportunistically conceived, essentially experimental, works on the other. By "opportunistically" I simply mean seizing upon the creatively available, *en disponibilité*—as when Faulkner speaks of having begun such novels as *The Sound and the Fury* and *Light in August* with little sense of the course they would eventually follow. Thus *Flags in the Dust (Sartoris)* is succeeded by *The Sound and the Fury, The Sound and the Fury* by *Sanctuary I* (the original version), *Sanctuary I* by *As I Lay Dying, As I Lay Dying* by *Sanctuary II* (the published version), *Sanctuary II* by *Light in August*. So far so good, but (if short stories and poems are set aside) the sequence then runs *Light in August/Pylon, Pylon/Absalom, Absalom!* before returning more neatly (for my present purposes) to *Absalom, Absalom!/The Unvanquished, The Unvanquished/The Wild Palms,* and *The Wild Palms/The Hamlet.*

Whether any significant, discussible pattern does in fact exist I'm not at all sure. After all, the short stories of these years (which cover the publication of *These 13* and *Doctor Martino*) are so important and so numerous that they cannot properly be ignored; it is also possible that Faulkner devoted more time than we now realize to the working out of his first conception of *Requiem for a Nun*. And of course there are other qualifications to be registered: *As I Lay Dying,* for all the self-consciousness of its technique, may well have originated in a Yoknapatawphan tall tale (Faulkner always insisted that he "knew from the first" [15] where the book was going), and there can be no doubt of the stylistic sophistication of *The Hamlet.* But the pattern to which I have tentatively pointed does at least suggest that Faulkner felt a tension—what he might have called a counterpoint—between these two strands in his work, and that at this particular period he was being driven headlong forward not so much by the desire to stake and develop his claim to Yoknapatawpha County as by what Yeats called the "fascination of what's difficult." [16] To such an extent, indeed, that during the great culminating act of his experimentalism, the writing of *Absalom, Absalom!,* Faulkner sought resolution and release not in the completion of one of his initial Yoknapatawphan conceptions but in the rapid, straight-from-scratch composition of *Pylon,* a specifically non-Yoknapatawphan exercise based on recent events in his own personal experience and possessing technical and intellectual affinities to *Absalom, Absalom!* itself.

Perhaps I'm not saying more than that Faulkner seems to have had, following *The Sound and the Fury,* two creative agendas: the original Yoknapatawphan agenda, which called for the progressive literary colonization of his imagined world, and another, less predictable because altogether more peremptory, which required him to realize to the fullest possible extent his personal potential as an artist. Of the imperiousness of Faulkner's ambitions, his need and determination to match himself against the greatest of novelists and the most intractable of technical problems, there can surely be no doubt, and it's therefore unsurprising that this second, self-testing, experimentalist agenda, though increasingly set aside during Faulkner's later years, should at periods of the greatest creative urgency have tended to take precedence over everything else. Asked at the University of Virginia why *The Town* had taken him so long to finish, Faulkner first characterized the book as a chronicle rather than as a novel and then explained:

There were so many other things that got in the way of it. I would write a little on it and then I would think of something else that seemed more urgent, that did fit into the more or less rigid pattern which a novel has got to conform to and this was too loose to fit into that form to give the pleasure which doing a complete job within the rules of the craft demand. That it's more fun doing a single piece which has the unity and coherence, the proper emphasis and integration, which a long chronicle doesn't have. That was the reason. Though it had to be done before I did stop writing.[17]

The job had to be done because it was an integral part of the expansive Yoknapatawphan project with which his career proper had begun. But because it offered only a relatively minor technical challenge, hence only relatively minor creative rewards, it was a job that had again and again been pushed to one side.

The most famous constitutional document of the Faulknerian kingdom is of course the *Paris Review* interview with Jean Stein, concluding with that richly stuffed final paragraph (favorite recourse of academics in want of a title) about the "little postage stamp of native soil," the "cosmos of my own," and so forth.[18] I quoted a sentence from it early in this paper and I'm sure that any randomly assembled group of Faulknerians could—perhaps do—stand together and recite it like a creed. But it must not be forgotten that the words of that paragraph were not spoken (or perhaps written) until 1955, long after the creative episodes to which they refer. It was yet two years more, indeed, before Faulkner spoke of the moment when he saw everything at once as in a lightning flash. A rather different set of imperatives emerges from the unused prefaces to *The Sound and the Fury* that Faulkner drafted in the early 1930s—documents written much sooner after the event, much closer to the front line, and recording with extraordinary sharpness what was clearly nothing short of a second epiphanic experience, no less powerful or important than the first:

> I wrote this book [*The Sound and the Fury*] and learned to read. I had learned a little about writing from Soldiers'

Pay—how to approach language, words: not with seriousness so much, as an essayist does, but with a kind of alert respect, as you approach dynamite; even with joy, as you approach women: perhaps with the same secretly unscrupulous intentions. But when I finished The Sound and The Fury I discovered that there is actually something to which the shabby term Art not only can, but must, be applied. I discovered then that I had gone through all that I had ever read, from Henry James through Henty to newspaper murders, without making any distinction or digesting any of it, as a moth or a goat might. After The Sound and The Fury and without heeding to open another book and in a series of delayed repercussions like summer thunder, I discovered the Flauberts and Dostoievskys and Conrads whose books I had read ten years ago. With The Sound and The Fury I learned to read and quit reading, since I have read nothing since.[19]

Those allusions to the "delayed repercussions like summer thunder" nicely (for my purposes) suggest that it was only with the writing of *The Sound and the Fury* that Faulkner realized the full implications of that earlier lightning flash. As *Sartoris* (*Flags in the Dust*) had somewhat cumbersomely shown, regionalism in and of itself was not enough: at some point "the shabby term Art" had to be invoked. And in the same piece Faulkner obliquely acknowledged that the writing of *Sanctuary* was a throwback to that earlier period and manner: "that part of me which learned as I wrote, which perhaps is the very force which drives a writer to the travail of invention and the drudgery of putting seventy-five or a hundred thousand words on paper, was absent [during the writing of *Sanctuary*] because I was still reading by repercussion the books which I had swallowed whole ten years and more ago."[20]

It is true that Faulkner went on to lament that the "ecstasy" experienced in writing *The Sound and the Fury* had not recurred even with *As I Lay Dying* and *Light in August* and would never return again.[21] But that was said before the writing of *Absalom, Absalom!*, when perhaps the ecstasy did return for him—as something approximating to ecstasy miraculously recurs for the reader at each new reading—and the lamentation needs in any case to be set alongside a passage from the other, evidently earlier, draft preface (dated 19 August 1933) in which Faulkner declared that, even if that ecstasy had gone forever, "[t]he unreluctance to begin, the cold satisfaction in work well and arduously done, is there and will continue to be there as long as I can do it well."[22] In that phrase about work not just "well" but "arduously done" Faulkner put into his own words that fascination with what's difficult, that need of the artist to meet the self-posed challenge, that is fundamental to the distinction I have been trying to draw. And in "cold satisfaction" he identified the kind of unyielding determination that was later to enable—and to oblige—him to bring *A Fable* finally to the point of publication, an effort that figures as but one item in the bibliographical record but that needs to be reckoned, in terms of sheer expenditure of creative energy, as equivalent to several of those less demanding (which is not in the least to say unserious or even "minor") Yoknapatawphan completions and reworkings that otherwise dominated the latter part of his career.

It would of course be highly artificial to attempt to draw a dividing line between Faulkner as artist and Faulkner as regionalist. All his major works were written within a regional context, even the deliberately non-Yoknapatawphan fiction—*Pylon, The Wild Palms*, and *A Fable*—being in some sense defined and "placed" by his and our awareness of that context, even as those novels contributed, by their very distinctiveness, to the definition of Yoknapatawpha. The community of the novels as regional works lends them a distinctive group identity that is crucial to their quasi-pastoral function, provides a powerful inducement to the reader to move on from one text to another (as Scott and Hardy had earlier realized), and insists that they be read not just individually but also in terms of their interrelationships.

And nothing Faulkner wrote—nothing, at least, that he offered within the covers of a book—was allowed, as he put it in the introduction to *Sanctuary*, to "shame" his best work. It remains, even so, a valuable exercise to think in terms of two distinct moments of vision and the two consequent agendas, and to recognize the roughly ten-year period from the late 1920s to the late 1930s when Faulkner's passionate need for self-development and self-challenge as an artist took precedence over his specifically regionalist and world-creating ambitions. It is also interesting to speculate that the demon then driving him, the gadfly of this most impetuous phase of his whole impetuous career, derived much of its coercive power (as Judith Wittenberg first showed)[23] from personal and psychological sources.

Six of the eight novels of those years were set in Yoknapatawpha and so rendered capable of drawing upon settings established in earlier novels, Faulkner having already allowed himself to assume that the reader of each novel would be—at any rate should be—familiar with all of its predecessors. In the longer run, of course, those same novels contributed to the process of regional elaboration, but that was clearly not the main thrust of at least the major works of the period, nor did their localizing features always conform to pre-existing Yoknapatawphan patterns: the Jefferson of *Light in August*, for example, seemed less like the Jefferson of *Sartoris* (and later of *Requiem* and the Snopes novels) than did the Charlestown, Georgia, of *Soldiers' Pay*. And it is possible to suspect that the insertion of the first Yoknapatawpha map into the first edition of *Absalom, Absalom!* constituted not so much an act of regionalist assertion as a further supplementation of that series of enigmatic appendices that begins with a grossly inaccurate chronology and continues with an excessively informative genealogy.

To think of the entirety of Faulkner's work as laid out as on a map, as existing on a single plane, is of course one way of resolving or at any rate circumventing the issues I have been trying to consider. Since the career is, after all, finished, no longer in motion, what harm can there be in arranging its individual components like features on a map, pieces on a board, figures in a design? No harm at all, obviously, in purely critical terms, though it soon begins to seem necessary to turn the map into a relief map, supply its contours with a third dimension, in order to give adequate recognition to the relative stature of the various works as well as to the nature of their intertextuality, the narrative, structural, fabular, or symbolic play among them. Ultimately, of course, the critic, the reader, can impose upon, read into, Faulkner's career any shape his or her knowledge, intelligence, or urge for singularity may dictate—to the point of deciding that Faulkner himself is irrelevant to the entire discussion, that the works essentially wrote themselves.

Coming to Faulkner's work with my own biographical, genetic, and chronological biases, however, I cannot help thinking of his career, as he lived and worked it through—pursuing that swift-running course as of the sun or a star through the heavens—as having a dynamic of its own, one that may not always have been consistent either in its operation or in its direction but that it seems interesting, and important, and even necessary to come to terms with in some way. At present the principles of its operation remain mysterious. Doubtless we shall gain more insight into the matter as we come to understand more, critically, about the intricate relationships that seem to exist among so many of Faulkner's texts, early and late, major and minor, finished and unfinished. Perhaps, when the surviving Faulkner manuscripts and letters have been more fully explored, we shall learn more about the genetic interdependence of certain texts and hence about the factors that determined the particular timing of their completion and publication. Just how did *Sanctuary* relate to *The Sound and the Fury*? Or *Light in August* to *Absalom, Absalom!*, both at one stage entitled *Dark House*, both owing a debt to "Evangeline"—much as "The Big Shot" was drawn upon both for *Light in August* and for *Sanctuary*? How did the composition of other texts during the evolution of *A Fable* affect, negatively or positively, the progress of the latter? Was *The Reivers*, that charmingly appropriate act of closure, in any sense consciously written as its author's final word? In the meantime we can continue to read with speculative sympathy the extraordinary textual legacy of Faulkner's tumultuous, unresting career—certain only that, to quote from *Go Down, Moses*, it was "a fine race while it lasted, but the tree was too quick."[24]

"A Cosmos of My Own": The Evolution of Yoknapatawpha

I have already invoked the words in which Faulkner recalled his original conception of his fictional world as a moment of instantaneous revelation: "I thought of the whole story at once like a bolt of lightning lights up a landscape and you see everything."[1] But because it seems such an important statement, in its insistence upon the primacy of a landscape as well as upon the suddenness and comprehensiveness of the vision itself, I want to explore its implications a little further, to consider the origins of Yoknapatawpha County in both general and specific terms, and to try and determine in what ways and with what consequences Yoknapatawpha changed in conception and realization over the years that followed.

We do not yet know—we may never know—just when Faulkner experienced that originary moment. In his prefatory note to *The Mansion*, first published in 1959, he spoke of that novel as the conclusion and summation of "a work conceived and begun in 1925."[2] Faulkner was rarely precise about dates—they seem to have ranked high among those facts that, as he so often declared, didn't much interest him—but this date is twice insisted upon within the one brief note and seems worth pondering a little. It is true that the Snopeses, who were absolutely central to his vision, don't seem to have been invented until the Spotted Horses material was first worked up into "Father Abraham," perhaps in 1926, possibly a little later. James B. Meriwether has argued, however, that the Snopeses had their origin in the Al Jackson tall tales which Faulkner swapped with Sherwood Anderson in New Orleans in 1925,[3] and it seems likely enough that in bringing the story of the Snopeses to an end in *The Mansion* Faulkner would have been ready to pay tribute not only to his friend and early supporter Phil Stone—to whom all three of the Snopes novels are dedicated—but also to Sherwood Anderson, co-creator of Al Jackson and dedicatee of *Sartoris*, the first published work in which the Snopeses appeared. (The *Sartoris* dedication, incidentally, is a characteristic Faulknerian mixture of compliment and arrogance—"*To Sherwood Anderson through whose kindness I was first published, with the belief that this book will give him no reason to regret that fact*"[4]—and it's possible that Faulkner, who had parodied Anderson before, was making gentle fun of Anderson's own somewhat self-regarding dedication to *Winesburg, Ohio*: "To the memory of my mother Emma Smith Anderson whose keen observations on the life about her first awoke in me the hunger to see beneath the surface of lives, this book is dedicated.")[5]

That Faulkner was deeply aware of the part Anderson had played in showing him the way to his own literary ground is indicated by a number of close correspondences between the familiar passage on Yoknapatawpha in the *Paris Review* interview of 1955 and the essay on Anderson that Faulkner had written for the *Atlantic Monthly* just a year or so previously. Faulkner recalled in that essay the advice Anderson had given him back in 1925: " 'You have to have somewhere to start from: then you begin to learn,' he told me. 'It dont matter where it was, just so you remember it and aint ashamed of it. Because one place to start from is just as important as any other. You're a country boy; all you know is that little patch up there in Mississippi where you started from. But that's all right too. It's America too; pull it out, as little and unknown as it is, and the whole thing will collapse, like when you prize a brick out of a wall.'"[6] Here, clearly, are the origins of those famous Faulknerian phrases about the little postage stamp of native soil and the created world that he liked to think of "as being a kind of keystone in the Universe; that, as small as that keystone is, if it were ever taken away, the universe itself would collapse."[7] Faulkner quarrelled at the time with Anderson's image of the brick pulled out of the wall—"'Not a cemented, plastered wall,' I said"[8]—and improved upon that image by using the keystone idea when speaking of his own work later on. But that did not detract from the actual acknowledgment of indebtedness to Anderson, less perhaps for the advice— which Faulkner arguably didn't really need—than for his example, especially in *Winesburg, Ohio*.

The importance of *Winesburg* for Faulkner is suggested by its subtitle, *A Group of Tales of Ohio Small Town Life*, its focus on a small rural community, and its portrayal of that community's life in a series of episodes sufficiently independent for some of them to have been separately published yet clearly interrelated both as vignettes of the town and as juxtaposed parables, chapters in the Book of the Grotesque. Nor can Faulkner have missed the presence, on the inside front cover of the first edition, of a sketch-map of the fictional town. That map—together, no doubt, with maps of Hardy's Wessex, Stevenson's Treasure Island, and so on—was perhaps as important to Faulkner as anything else. It is a typical approach of the regionalist to work with existing geography but make it his own through the invention of new names and the relocation of places and buildings in order to suit his artistic convenience. So Hardy superimposed his fictional Wessex upon the actual geography of southwestern England, making up names for the towns and villages in which the action of his stories took place but retaining the real names of places on the periphery of his region as a way of establishing a generalized sense of location and authenticity. So, too, Faulkner refers to such cities as Memphis and New Orleans as places to which it is possible to go from Yoknapatawpha, even though in *The Hamlet* the inhabitants of Frenchman's Bend are unable to answer the Texan's inquiry as to the short way to New York.

Faulkner's realization in print of the potentialities of his own region began, as he says in the *Paris Review* interview, with *Sartoris*, that abbreviated version of *Flags in the Dust* first published early in 1929. There was no map in *Sartoris*—that was not to come until *Absalom, Absalom!*, when Faulkner was a more established figure—but he clearly had in his mind, perhaps even on paper on the table beside him as he wrote, at least an outline of what at this point he still seems to have been calling Yocona County.[9] A strong visual image of the region is created in the novel, distances are given, towns and houses described in some detail. We learn about the agriculture of the region, its climate through the course of the full annual cycle, its social, economic, and racial structure, something of its history and characteristic activities. Faulkner, in short, was staking out his territorial claim, and with such deliberateness and at such length that he would not need to do the job again—despite his apparent reimagination of Jefferson as corresponding more closely to Oxford, Mississippi, than to the Ripley, Mississippi, identifiably reflected in *Sartoris* itself. There is, indeed, a real sense in which later novels such as *Sanctuary*, *The Sound and the Fury*, and *Light in August* are partly dependent upon the reader's assumed familiarity with the earlier work.

Immediately at issue here, of course, is the whole question of the relationship of Faulkner's Yoknapatawpha novels one to another. He stressed in his later years the importance of an overall design, and he seems to have appreciated early on the need for something more complex than Hardy's rather two-dimensional Wessex—of which, as I shall indicate later, he was almost certainly aware. It is evident, too, that his mind at this period was running much on the example of Balzac: he mentioned two of Balzac's recurring characters in the course of the article on Sherwood Anderson he wrote for the *Dallas Morning News* in April 1925. His comments on Balzac are always appreciative, and in the *Paris Review* interview he speaks, in an especially revealing phrase, of Balzac's having "created an intact world of his own, a bloodstream running through twenty books." [10] The precision of that figure "twenty," a significant underestimate of Balzac's total production, doubtless had more than a little to do with Faulkner's having published, at the time of the interview, exactly twenty fiction volumes of his own.

Ambitious as he obviously was for an intact world, a bloodstream running through all his own work, Faulkner must have contemplated very early on the Balzacian example of a systematically organized fictional world in which a long series of socially designated texts (e.g., novels of Parisian life, provincial life, etc.), populated by numerous recurring characters, serves to demonstrate the complex interconnectedness of all classes of society and the persistence throughout of the same patterns of human folly. And while Faulkner did not in practice adopt such a scheme, its traces may still be discernible in the socioeconomic structuring of *Flags in the Dust* and *Sartoris,* in the intricately sordid interconnections—political, economic, sexual—among the different social layers of *Sanctuary,* and in the thematic and narrative continuities linking *Sanctuary* to *Flags in the Dust* and to the short story "There Was a Queen." As I shall argue later, those same continuities were apparently to have been sustained in *Requiem for a Nun,* projected at that early time though not brought to completion until 1951. Add to this the extended backward glance of *The Unvanquished.* Add, too, the pervasive infestation of these texts by Snopeses and the potential incorporation of the entire body of Snopes narratives, both written and as yet unwritten. Add all these elements and one begins to get some sense of the ambitiousness—perhaps even the specifically Balzacian ambitiousness—of Faulkner's design in its early stages.

Not included in that reckoning, even so, is the wide-ranging body of material centered, at least in technical terms, upon the figure of Quentin Compson. Quentin, it's worth remembering, is the narrator not only of the Compson story, "That Evening Sun," but also of "Lion," one of the principal starting points of what eventually became *Go Down, Moses,* and of "A Justice," in which he hears from Sam Fathers the tale of Indian times relating specifically to Sam's own birth. Although not identified by name, Quentin may also at some stage have been cast as the narrator of some of those early stories in which the voice of the town, of the local community, is invoked—"A Rose for Emily," for example. He was certainly to have been the residual narrator, the recording recipient, of the episode involving Ab Snopes's defeat by the horse-trader Pat Stamper that was published in *Scribner's Magazine* as the V. K. Suratt story "Fool about a Horse" and incorporated into *The Hamlet* as an extended anecdote told by V. K. Ratliff—Suratt renamed and to some extent reconceived. Two other Suratt/Ratliff stories must also have been Quentin Compson narratives: "Spotted Horses," absorbed into *The Hamlet* as the omnisciently told episode of the auction of the Texas horses, and "A Bear Hunt," another story on the fringes of *Go Down, Moses* territory.[11]

Faulkner's use of the device of the framed narrative, the story told within a story or within a particularized conditioning context, is understandable enough in itself. His imagination had from boyhood been seized by the stories—of hunting, Indians, the Civil War, Reconstruction, the deeds of local heroes and villains, including members of his own family—that he had heard over and over again from the lips of his elders, both white and black, and there can be no question but that such tales were a major element in the growth of his awareness of the potentialities of his own region as a subject for fiction. If that awareness came in the form of a single overwhelming shock of recognition, then such tales must have been salient features of that suddenly illuminated landscape, their exploitability precisely what was recognized. One of Faulkner's earliest instincts as a writer, even before Yoknapatawpha, was to exploit the oral tale, and especially the traditional tall tale, as a basis for written narrative. But while such a method served well enough for primarily humorous purposes—in the Al Jackson stories, for example, and "Father Abraham"—it was less adaptable to those wider, richer, and often more somber undercurrents he soon learned to recognize in many of the tales he wanted to relate. By inserting a hearer or intervener such as Quentin, however, someone with assumptions, instincts, and sensitivities quite different from those of the tale-teller himself, it became immediately possible to bring those other aspects closer to the surface. In "A Justice," for example, the story of Sam Fathers's birth is recounted in comic terms, but the presence of Quentin, brooding upon something he would fully understand only when he had grown older ("passed on and through and beyond the suspension of twilight"),[12] serves to retrieve for the reader some sense of what the narrated events would have meant for those involved—what they must still mean, in personal and racial terms, for Sam himself.

Faulkner's reasons for using a narrator such as Quentin were thus practical enough. But in making Quentin the recipient of so many tales from so many different sources, he clearly had something more in mind. Earlier novelists who had used framing devices had often employed them for sequences of narratives rather than for single works, and Faulkner, who would certainly have been familiar with the precedents established by, for example, Scott and Hawthorne, seems clearly to have intended Quentin to fill some structural and indeed specifically regional role. In "A Justice" Quentin is accompanied by a family group made up of his sister and brother, Caddy and Jason Compson, his grandfather, General Compson, and one of the family's black servants, Roskus; as in "That Evening Sun" there is no mention of Benjy. In surviving manuscript and typescript versions of the "Fool about a Horse" material, Quentin listens to Suratt's tale as one of a group consisting of General Compson, Roskus, and Doc Peabody. The latter, of course, provides a link with the worlds of *Sartoris (Flags in the Dust)* and *As I Lay Dying*, and his presence in this particular context tends to confirm one's sense of the tight interrelatedness of Faulkner's initial design. As for Quentin himself, I strongly suspect that he was at one stage intended to function as the essential recording figure within variant forms of this same framing situation deployed through a whole series of otherwise distinct narratives. In looking back from the perspective of adulthood upon the tales he had heard as a child, he was presumably to have learned to appreciate not only their intrinsic human significance but also their particular meaning for him as a boy and man of his place and time—to recognize them, in short, as quintessential expressions of the regional world, past and present, that had made him what he was.

In this respect it is, I think, quite proper to suggest, as critics have already done, that Quentin is in at least some texts a semi-autobiographical figure whose listening to the tales of the past had its basis in Faulkner's own experience. Just how ambitious a structural role was once envisioned for him can now only be guessed at. It is, of course, possible that he was never intended to be anything more than a convenient device for grouping together and loosely unifying a series of miscellaneous stories—such as the "collections of short stories of my townspeople" Faulkner mentioned to Horace Liveright in February 1927.[13] But the available evidence seems sufficient to suggest that Quentin was once perceived as a focal point—though not necessarily the only one—for the Compson material, the Snopes/Surratt material (the scheme had already evaporated by the time Ratliff appeared), and for what subsequently became the Sam Fathers/hunting/McCaslin material. The Sartoris/Benbow material seems to have been kept quite separate, though linked to the overall Yoknapatawpha pattern by means of such overlapping characters as Doc Peabody and some of the Snopeses.

It seems probable, in fact, that when (in 1926 or thereabouts) Faulkner first embarked on a Sartoris novel and a Snopes novel more or less simultaneously, he deliberately chose quite different narrative methods for the two projects. In *Sartoris* (*Flags in the Dust*), as in the closely connected *Sanctuary*, the point of view was omniscient: while discrete narrative episodes such as the tales told by Will Falls and the Memphis adventures of Vergil and Fonzo might be included, they were consistently absorbed within the prevailing narrative flow. With the Snopes material, on the other hand, Faulkner seems to have decided, if not at the very beginning then shortly afterward, to allow the separate narratives not only to retain but to proclaim their individuality, to have them told as self-contained units and in specifically regional and often dialectal voices, and to tie them together in terms of their common and no doubt cumulative impact upon the sensitive imagination and educated mind of Quentin Compson—who was (like the author himself) ineluctably of the South and yet capable of seeing it, or of trying to see it, in wider, nonregional perspectives.

Before leaving Quentin I want to ponder for a moment the possible implications of Faulkner's having once given the title "As I Lay Dying" to a short story version (never published) of the closing stages of the Spotted Horses episode,[14] the sequel to the auction itself. It seems on the face of it an absurdly inappropriate title, much better (if still somewhat confusingly) applied to the novel for which Faulkner used it a little later on. But if it is possible to understand his once calling "Spotted Horses" itself "Aria con amore"[15] as a gesture of personal or narratorial love and commitment toward the regional material or toward the horses themselves as embodiments of energy, sexuality, and above all creativity, then it is surely possible to look for some explanation for that "As I Lay Dying" title as well. We know that the words "as I lay dying" formed part of a longer quotation from the *Odyssey* that Faulkner was fond of reciting: "As I lay dying the woman with the dog's eyes would not close my eyelids for me as I descended into Hades."[16] What is interesting in the present context is the appearance of a fragment of that same quotation ("*the woman with the dog's eyes*") in "Carcassonne," [17] a story about creative vision and inspiration that was obviously of special private significance for Faulkner—and can be linked to the Spotted Horses material through the passage in which a buckskin pony becomes a Pegasus-like symbol of ambitious creativity. The poet-narrator of "Carcassonne" is evidently dying himself ("As I Lay Dying" would have been an appropriate alternative title), and it seems feasible to infer that Quentin was at some point projected as a dying narrator whose whole world would pass before his eyes in almost instantaneous review (as is said to be the experience of those who drown), thus reflecting or reenacting Faulkner's own instantaneous and comprehensive vision of Yoknapatawpha. Technically, of course, that review would consist of a series of regional narrations linked by Quentin's presence as auditor and recorder.

Quentin does, of course, drown in *The Sound and the Fury,* and his whole section could be, and has been, spoken of as just such a dying flashback. Interestingly, it is a flashback full of voices, of remembered conversation and speech, chiefly Mr. Compson's but also Caddy's and Shreve's and several others'. In *Absalom, Absalom!* Quentin is torn apart by the various conflicting voices juxtaposed within his memory, and it is possible to see in that novel the ultimate realization, what Faulkner himself might have called the apotheosis, of just the kind of retrospective, reevaluating role that Quentin was originally invented to perform—though made much more complex, and much more somber, as a consequence of Faulkner's increased maturity both as man and as artist. One can even think of the entire novel, deliberately located by Faulkner just a few months before that suicide of which *The Sound and the Fury* has already informed us, as constituting Quentin's drowning flashback—and of those desperate concluding words about the South ("*I dont hate it! I dont hate it!*") [18] as embodying his final thoughts as he goes down for the last time. One *can* think this, although, as I shall argue later, I'm not at all sure that one should.

The irony in all this is that by the time *Absalom* was written and published, any such comprehensive structuring had long been shattered beyond repair, most obviously by Faulkner's having killed off Quentin in *The Sound and the Fury*—even though that did not prevent his occasionally re-using Quentin, unnamed, as a convenient narrative perspective: thus the unidentified narrator of "The Old People" (as published in *Harper's* for September 1940) is the same person to whom Sam Fathers told the story of "A Justice." But if that pattern was indeed conceived in retrospective terms—and *Sartoris (Flags in the Dust)* and the various stories narrated by Quentin all look back at the past from the vantage point of the narrative present—it was in any case doomed to eventual destruction by its failure to make allowance for the author's own existence in time, for the likelihood of his continuing to live and write on into the future, beyond the frozen moment, whenever it was originally intended to be, of Quentin's death. Backward and past-obsessed though it might seem and be, even Yoknapatawpha, even northern Mississippi, could not remain motionless and unchanging. This was something Faulkner came to understand very clearly in later years, when the concept of life as motion became central to his thought and his work, and that understanding was no doubt sharpened and confirmed, within his own creative experience, by the way in which Yoknapatawpha itself had so rapidly and so radically burst the bonds of its initial time- and map-bound conception.

This is not necessarily to suggest that it was for these reasons that Faulkner abandoned that conception—or, indeed, that he abandoned it on any clearly perceived or deliberately calculated grounds. To determine just what happened, and when, one would need to solve what is still the most intriguing of the many creative mysteries in Faulkner's career: How did he come to write *The Sound and the Fury*? My own guess would be that the crucial moment occurred when he first thought of Benjy as the unidentified narrator of an already written third-person short story about the Compson children on the night of their grandmother's death. In any case, the new departure, whenever it came and wherever it came from, was almost certainly technical in nature, involving a realization of the potentialities inherent in point of view, in the multiplicity of points of view, and in the combination of such multiplicity with the manipulation, the resonating juxtaposition, of discrete structural units. Faulkner had already chosen his material, decided what it was he wanted to write about. Then, as he recalled in 1933 in an unpublished introduction to *The Sound and the Fury*, he discovered for the first time the excitement of writing itself: "I said to myself, Now I can write. Now I can make myself a vase like that which the old Roman kept at his bedside and wore the rim slowly away with kissing it." [19]

I am rashly positing, in short, two supreme moments of discovery in Faulkner's career: the first, the moment when he perceived the whole rich prospect of his fictional county extended before him; the second, the moment when he perceived the infinite possibilities inherent in the diligent exercise and fearless extension of the fictional techniques already pioneered by such writers as James and Conrad and Joyce. If there was a third such moment it perhaps occurred when he achieved, in *The Hamlet*, the perfect marriage that resulted from a return to his original subject matter equipped with the technical wisdom gained from the experimentation of the late 1920s and early 1930s.

While that experimentation was so absorbingly in progress, Faulkner's Yoknapatawphan schemes fell distinctly into abeyance, to the point that the publication of the first Yoknapatawpha map in the first edition of *Absalom, Absalom!* seemed less the culmination of a developing process than a rather arbitrary reassertion of a claim fallen somewhat into public disrepair, a way of insisting that all the new books and locations and characters could indeed be absorbed into the original scheme—find, at the very least, a place on the map. In some respects, the erosion of the pattern was irreversible. It is true that Faulkner spoke sometime in the early 1930s of his eventual need to make his collected works consistent one with another. It is also true that toward the end of his life he made gestures toward achieving some kind of narrative consistency within the Snopes trilogy. But that attempt was abandoned when he realized that it would be a matter not just of adjusting the details of *The Mansion* to fit with those of *The Hamlet* and *The Town* but of revising *The Hamlet* and *The Town* in accordance with the matured vision of the later novel.[20] That prefatory note to *The Mansion* at once reflects the experience and justifies its outcome: "[T]he purpose of this note is simply to notify the reader that the author has already found more discrepancies and contradictions than he hopes the reader will—contradictions and discrepancies due to the fact that the author has learned, he believes, more about the human heart and its dilemma than he knew thirty-four years ago; and is sure that, having lived with them that long time, he knows the characters in this chronicle better than he did then." [21]

Life as motion indeed. Faulkner began with a plan, evidently conceived in the essentially two-dimensional terms of a landscape, a map. Then he seems to have laid aside the plan for a while, in what can perhaps be best called a burst of creative ecstasy, until a moment came when he suddenly found that he had a world on his hands. The original concept, he said in the *Paris Review* interview, opened up a gold mine of other people—or peoples: there is an unresolved textual crux at this point, but I assume he meant that the concept proved more richly generative than he had ever imagined. So, he continued, "I created a cosmos of my own." [22] A cosmos: an "ordered" world, as dictionary definitions insist, but not a rigidly systematic one, for the order in question is that which is synonymous with harmony, exists in time as well as in space, and is therefore capable always of growth and change. As Faulkner concisely put it in the same interview: "I can move these people around like God, not only in space but in time too." [23]

In claiming such total power in relation to his created universe, Faulkner was really saying all that need be said on the question of inconsistencies as between one book and another. When he reintroduced into such late novels as *The Mansion* and *The Reivers* characters who had not otherwise appeared in his work since 1930 or thereabouts, that did not mean that he himself had lost sight of them in the meantime. Like all his other characters they had always been there, waiting in what Faulkner liked to call the attic, ready to make another public appearance—probably with a somewhat refurbished act—whenever called upon to do so. Faulkner's whole world seems to have remained perpetually alive and active in his imagination, as something quite apart from his capacity, as a time-bound human being, to realize that world on paper. There is plenty of evidence to suggest that not only large patterns of narrative development but detailed scenes and incidents were fully conceived and worked out in his mind years before he actually got around to writing them down. And his comments in interviews about characters in books written years before, and apparently not reread in the interim, show how vividly they remained present to him.

Yoknapatawpha is thus, to an extraordinary degree, a conceptually unified world, growing progressively, harmoniously, and ever more richly out of a single original idea. But it is also, and for the same reasons, an infinitely fluid world, in which the maturing creative imagination of the author is under no obligation to observe a rigid consistency in such matters as geography, chronology, or characterization. Thus we should not be surprised or disturbed that Faulkner seems to have shifted the location of Jefferson, that the time scheme of the Snopes trilogy is something less than exact (it is a rare novelist, incidentally, who can get the chronology even of a single novel absolutely correct), or that the recurrence of a named character does not necessarily mean that he or she will behave in precisely the same fashion on each occasion, or even have exactly the same personal history.

These matters would doubtless have become clearer had Faulkner lived to complete that "Golden Book" of Yoknapatawpha County of which he speaks at the very end of the *Paris Re-*

view interview: "My last book will be the Doomsday Book, the Golden Book, of Yoknapatawpha County. Then I shall break the pencil and I'll have to stop."[24] As James B. Meriwether has pointed out, by "Golden Book" Faulkner probably had in mind the ancient genealogical register of the nobility of Venice, and Joseph Blotner describes in his biography of Faulkner a brief manuscript, dated 1932, that is headed "The Golden Book of Jefferson & Yoknapatawpha County in Mississippi" and contains a seven-hundred-word biography of John Sartoris.[25] The Compson "Appendix"—first written for Malcolm Cowley's *Portable Faulkner*—is evidently the best published approximation to what Faulkner seems to have had in mind, emerging as it plainly does from a desire to assert his sense of absolute proprietorship over his world and to endow his characters in public, as it were, with those personal and family histories they had so long possessed in the privacy of his own mind. Faulkner also uses the term Doomsday Book, almost as if he foresaw some final day of judgment he would visit upon his own creation—godlike, or at least Prospero-like, since that threatened breaking of his pencil sounds suspiciously like an allusion to Prospero's burning of his books.

Since, however, Doomsday Book is invoked interchangeably with Golden Book, he must have been thinking chiefly of the economic survey of England undertaken in the eleventh century immediately following the Norman Conquest, though perhaps also of *Domesday Book*, a long poem by Edgar Lee Masters that recounts, from multiple points of view, the story of a coroner's investigation into the death of a young woman. "A word now on the Domesday book of old," writes Masters, with his bland blank verse and dubious etymology:

Of houses; domus, house, so domus book.
And this book of the death of Elenor Murray
Is not a book of doom, though showing too
How fate was woven round her, and the souls

That touched her soul; but it is a house book too
Of riches, poverty, and weakness, strength
Of this our country.[26]

The poem is thus offered both as "a census spiritual / Taken of our America" and as a demonstration of "The closeness of one life, however humble / With every life upon this globe."[27] Faulkner certainly knew Masters's work, and he seems to have projected his own Doomsday/Golden Book as a book of houses, of families, but his novels and stories everywhere explore the possibilities of human interconnectedness in ways far richer and more complex than Masters could ever have conceived. When Faulkner spoke in the *Paris Review* interview of sublimating the actual to apocryphal, he meant not making the true untrue but making the real symbolic, taking the stuff of everyday experience and refining it to the condition of legends or of what he liked to think of as fables, universally apprehensible embodiments of the eternal verities. The entire body of his fiction can in fact be read as a kind of Doomsday Book, a vast compendium of narrated tales and lives, of legends and speaking fables.

Asked in Japan about the creation of Yoknapatawpha, Faulkner first gave his usual reply—that it was simple, convenient, and economical to work with just one area—and then continued: "Or it may have been the same reason that is responsible for the long clumsy sentences and paragraphs. I was still trying to reduce my one individual experience of the world into one compact thing which could be picked up and held in the hands at one time."[28] Faulkner's ambition, early and late, was to make of his fictional world a dense distillation of the human world and its whole experience in time, a microcosmos capable of being looked at from all sides, contemplated whole and entire like a Grecian urn or that vase whose rim the old Roman wore slowly away with kissing—like the intact world he so much admired in Balzac, unlike the ultimately incoherent world he had found in Anderson who, he once said, seemed not to have had a "concept of a cosmos in miniature."[29] Faulkner was also, I believe, quite consciously seeking to create novels that would in their conceptual integrity and distinctively regional character be implicitly pastoral, in the sense in which John Lynen used that term in his fine study of Robert Frost[30]—as allowing basic human values and passions to emerge with unusual directness and simplicity and thus provide a standard or baseline by which those of us who live in more modern and complex societies can contemplate and evaluate our own conduct and assumptions.

Faulkner never realized on paper all that he had conceived in his imagination, and because he remained to the end of his career determined to explore new narrative techniques, nice questions of Yoknapatawphan consistency were always likely to take second place. For the reader there is nevertheless an unmistakable coherence to the Faulknerian *oeuvre*. The novels and stories illuminate, modify, and reinforce each other to a degree with which we have scarcely as yet begun to come to terms. And it is clear that for Faulkner himself Yoknapatawpha always retained as it grew and changed in his imagination an absolute integrity and reality. Asked in 1955 about his books being read and discussed all over the world, Faulkner replied that he liked it: "I like the idea of the world I created being a kind of keystone in the universe. Feel that if I ever took it away the universe around that keystone would crumble away. . . . If they believed in my world in America the way they do abroad, I could probably run one of my characters for President . . . maybe Flem Snopes."[31] Faulkner, as usual, was speaking only half-humorously, but it is not for a Canadian to ponder the appropriateness of his nominating Flem Snopes as the likeliest of his characters to succeed at the highest levels of American politics.

Faulkner's First Trilogy: *Sartoris,*
Sanctuary, and *Requiem for a Nun*

If my use of the term "trilogy" seems a little arbitrary
and even provocative at first glance, that is precisely because I want to prompt some rethinking of the relationships among the novels invoked. By exploring a little
further Faulkner's use of recurrent characters and situations in these specific instances I hope to arrive at a fuller
understanding of the interconnections among novels and
stories throughout the entire body of his work—a sharper
perception of the inner dynamics of a fictional world.
Not that the trilogy is just a convenient critical invention. There's an obvious continuity between *Flags in the
Dust* and *Sanctuary* on the one hand and a no less obvious overlap between *Sanctuary* and *Requiem for a Nun*
on the other. That there is any substantial connection
between the published *Sartoris* of 1929 and the published *Requiem* of 1951 may not be so clear, but there has
also to be fitted into the sequence the novel entitled *Requiem for a Nun* that Faulkner projected, and actually
started, in 1933.

The chronology is perhaps the first thing to get
straight, although as always in Faulkner studies it's wise

to avoid overconfident pronouncements on the basis of what may be an entirely accidental and unrepresentative survival of documentary evidence. We at any rate know that Faulkner wrote a novel entitled *Flags in the Dust* and that in November 1927 it was declined by Liveright, the publisher who had taken his first two novels, *Soldiers' Pay* and *Mosquitoes*. After adventures at which we can do little more than guess, that same novel was eventually accepted by Harcourt, Brace in September 1928, and published by them in January 1929 in a shortened form and under the new title of *Sartoris*. I should perhaps note here that because *Sartoris* was the only version of the text to achieve public visibility, hence referential status, during Faulkner's lifetime, it is the version to which I shall most often refer—thus conveniently dodging the awkwardness of *Flags/Sartoris*. (Since the publication of the Random House edition of *Flags in the Dust* in 1973 it has of course been possible to extend that formulation to *Flags/Sartoris/Flags*—though critics of the edition might prefer *Flags/Sartoris/Dust*.) The reduction of *Flags in the Dust* to the smaller dimensions of *Sartoris* was apparently carried out by Faulkner's friend and agent Ben Wasson, although it seems clear from the numerous passages of characteristically Faulknerian prose present in *Sartoris* but not in *Flags* that Faulkner either rewrote parts of the novel before Wasson went to work on it or made additions to the cut-down typescript, or to the galleys, before publication. The typescript sent to the printer seems not to have survived; if it had done so, of course, these and many other uncertainties surrounding the text could probably have been resolved.

At just the time when *Sartoris* was being published, Faulkner began writing the surviving manuscript of *Sanctuary*, which carries the dates January–May 1929. There is also a typescript bearing essentially the same dates, suggesting that Faulkner (as seems to have been his usual practice) typed up his work as he went along.[1] Between *Sartoris* and *Sanctuary* Faulkner had of course written *The Sound and the Fury*; by the time he got the galleys of *Sanctuary* he had also written *As I Lay Dying*, and it was his sense of creative achievement in those later texts that he subsequently offered as the explanation for the radical rewriting and restructuring of *Sanctuary* in which he engaged before the novel was finally published in February 1931. Curiously enough, the kind of surgery he performed was closely comparable to what Wasson had done to *Flags*, in that the tendency of the revision in both instances was to reduce the quantity and importance of the material relating to the Benbow family and hence shift the emphasis much more to the other major figure—Bayard Sartoris in *Sartoris*, Temple Drake in the published *Sanctuary*.

These two quite distinct acts of revision have together served to obscure the full intimacy of the connection between the original *Flags in the Dust* text and the original *Sanctuary* text—although "original" is of course a risky term to use in such a context. As I have suggested earlier, it's necessary to allow for the possibility that all the Benbow material once formed part of a larger pool of Sartoris-related material, comparable to Faulkner's early pool of Snopes material and at some level connected with it. Such a hypothesis allows for the further possibility that *Sanctuary*, although written after *The Sound and the Fury*, may have been conceived and drafted at least in outline at an earlier date. Faulkner said quite specifically on one occasion that he had written *Sanctuary* before *The Sound and the Fury*,[2] and while the context of that remark does not encourage its being thought of as one of Faulkner's most deliberate statements there are other, vaguer references to the same effect. Some of the central ideas of the novel—the bizarre rape, for example—were already in Faulkner's mind by the mid-1920s,[3] and the final scene of Temple in the Luxembourg Gardens seems to have originated in a "lost" short story written in Paris in 1925.[4] The hypothesis, however unproven, does at least offer a way of accounting for the technical conventionality of *Sanctuary*, otherwise so surprising in a work written in the immediate aftermath of *The Sound and the Fury*. On the other hand, *The Sound and the Fury* had not yet been accepted at the moment in January 1929 when Faulkner began work on the one *Sanctuary* manuscript that has actually survived, and he could well have returned to the mode and materials of *Sartoris* in the belief that they offered the best available road to commercial success—even while now investing them with something of the transformative creative exuberance that flowed directly from the experience of writing *The Sound and the Fury*.

It is at all events clear that Faulkner was ready to embark upon another Horace Benbow narrative—for the first (1929) version of *Sanctuary* is essentially that—just as soon as he had finished with *The Sound and the Fury* and seen *Sartoris* published. However commercial some of his motives may have been, it appears that they did not include a thrifty desire to use up material recently deleted from *Flags in the Dust*. Several direct references back to the world of *Flags* (and of *Sartoris*) occur in the *Sanctuary* manuscript and typescript, but many of these were omitted from the novel as finally published, and the small remainder alluded, almost without exception, to episodes and details that had, so to speak, been made public in *Sartoris*. Like any novelist beginning a book that was in some sense a sequel, Faulkner wanted to provide sufficient introductory information to new readers, those who had not read the earlier book, to enable them to approach its successor without difficulty or handicap. At the same time he seems to have wanted those who had read *Sartoris* not only to be aware of Horace, Narcissa, and so on as continuing characters but actually to be reminded of specific episodes in which they had been involved.

Early in the *Sanctuary* typescript, for example, we are told that Horace had returned home in the rain one day after Narcissa's marriage to Bayard and found her waiting for him:

> "Narcy," he said, "has that surly blackguard—?"
> "You fool! You fool! You haven't even an umbrella!"
> she said.[5]

This is obviously a condensation of a slightly longer scene at the end of the second chapter of part 4 of *Sartoris*, where Horace speaks precisely the words I have quoted but Narcissa calls him "idiot" twice instead of "fool" and complains that he has forgotten his raincoat.[6] It is an early instance of a phenomenon that recurs again and again in later works: Faulkner, making a deliberate retrospective allusion, either does not trouble to ensure its verbal accuracy or consciously chooses to adapt it, in language and content, to his current purposes. So Miss Quentin climbs down a pear tree in *The Sound and the Fury* and down a rainpipe in the Compson "Appendix." Faulkner of course defended such "inconsistencies" by declaring, in that prefatory note to *The Mansion*, that he had learned to know his characters better over the course of the years, and the practice was certainly in line with his profound sense, as man and artist, that life was motion, and motion life, that he must perpetually be posing and meeting new challenges rather than brooding upon the failures (as he always considered them) of the past.

In the particular instance of *Sanctuary* it is conceivable that Faulkner, distressed at the abandonment of the original conception of *Flags in the Dust* and especially at the deletion of so much Benbow family material, was initially concerned to make good some of the deficiencies of the published *Sartoris* by spelling out certain aspects of Horace's relationships with his sister Narcissa and with Belle Mitchell far more directly than he had done in *Sartoris*, or indeed in the uncut *Flags*. At one point in the *Sanctuary* typescript, for example, Horace recalls Belle's telling him that he was in love with Narcissa and adding, sardonically: "What do the books call it? What sort of complex?" Horace characteristically dodged the question by means of a feeble joke— "'Not complex,' he said. 'Do you think that any relation with her could be complex?'"[7]—but it is nevertheless possible to read the exchange as providing not just a reminder (or restatement for new readers) of an important aspect of *Sartoris* but also a commentary upon it, a clarification not entirely dissimilar to the "case-study" of Popeye that Faulkner inserted into the final version of *Sanctuary* itself.

But *Sanctuary* also comments, enlarges, depends upon *Sar-*

toris in a broader and deeper sense. Did it not do so it would be hard to see why Faulkner should have chosen to link the two novels so closely together. One of the central oppositions in *Sartoris* is between the American Civil War and World War I, between a specific time past and a no less precisely dated time present, the latter extending from the spring of 1919 to the early summer of 1920. In *Sanctuary*—especially in versions antedating the extensive deletion of Benbow material—the sections focused on Horace display a corresponding tension between past and present, where the present is identical with the date of composition of the novel, the immediate here and now, and the past with the time present of *Sartoris,* the postwar period when Bayard Sartoris came home, married Narcissa Benbow, and died and when Horace left Jefferson to go and live at Kinston in the Delta with Belle Mitchell.

Since the vision of existence that emerges from *Sanctuary* is much darker than the one that emerges from *Sartoris* it is possible to argue that Faulkner is offering in the later novel a statement about the deterioration of the world of Yoknapatawpha— and by implication of the actual world—during the period of the 1920s. But it might be equally feasible to argue that Faulkner, writing in 1929, was simply finding in the contemporary scene—specifically, in bootlegging and its connection to violence and organized crime—a convenient point of departure for a presentation of what might be called the other side of the world of *Sartoris,* a deliberate undercutting of the middle-class and agrarian values the earlier novel had appeared to offer as positives. I find my warrant for invoking such terms in a passage in the *Sanctuary* typescript in which Horace, overjoyed that Temple's disappearance from Miss Reba's has relieved him of the distressing responsibility of calling her as a witness, "realised again that furious homogeneity of the middle classes when opposed to the proletariat from which it is so recently sprung and by which it is so often threatened."[8] Although Faulkner did not choose to expose class issues so directly in the novel as published, the psychological and moral breakdown of Bayard Sartoris still finds its necessary counterpart not just in the poor white Byron Snopes but in such representative middle-class figures as the well-fed and well-educated lawyer Horace Benbow and the pampered coed Temple Drake. (Why Horace and Temple should be given the surnames of British admirals I do not know; Horace, indeed, also has the first name of an even more famous admiral, Nelson, and there was an earlier British admiral called Sartorius. Perhaps Faulkner took private pleasure in thinking of the spring in the opening scene of *Sanctuary* as a miniature sea across which Admiral Horatio Nelson Benbow found himself rudely confronted by Popeye the Sailor.)

Some of the impetus toward the composition of *Sanctuary* may again have derived from Faulkner's dissatisfaction with *Sartoris,* from which Horace emerges with rather more credit, or with less emphasized discredit, than he does from *Flags in the Dust.* But the main thrust is toward a deliberate revaluation and even inversion of the entire world of *Sartoris,* showing the Sartorises and Benbows and Drakes in their shabby and sometimes squalid relationships with each other, with people less fortunately born than themselves, and with the tentacular forces of corruption and violence. Horace, looking for a hill to lie on, might perhaps have been expected to find his way to the MacCallums. Instead he arrives at the Old Frenchman place and finds there a grotesque parody not just of the family farm but of the family itself: all the units necessary to a family are present, but all are in some way physically or socially maimed.[9] (I recognize that there are, as Albert Devlin pointed out,[10] some odd things about the MacCallums too.) What the reader learns to recognize is that however grotesque the ad hoc family at the Old Frenchman place may be—however offensive to the moral susceptibilities of the ladies of Jefferson—it nevertheless displays, in and through the person of Ruby Lamar, more vitality, more love, and certainly more warmth than anything Horace and Narcissa are capable of generating.

Narcissa, like Belle Mitchell, emerges badly from the comparison with Ruby and Miss Reba that is enforced throughout *Sanctuary* (e.g., in the link between the "rose colored shade" in Belle's bedroom and the "fluted shade of rose-colored paper" in Temple's room at Miss Reba's brothel),[11] and the later novel thus complements the earlier by making explicit, or at any rate evident, what had formerly only been hinted at. Taken together, the two novels present an essentially unitary view of a society increasingly subject to social corruption and moral decay, a world in which the young men are characteristically bent on self-destruction and the young women are technically or, what is worse, effectively whores. (It is true that any such categorization of Narcissa must be partly dependent upon the short story "There Was a Queen," published after *Sanctuary* but perhaps anticipated in the allusion to "the dead tranquil queens in stained marble"[12] in the novel's final paragraph and possibly intended at one time to be incorporated into the body of the text as an ironic counterpoint to Narcissa's persecution of Ruby, a woman who had also given herself sexually to a lawyer but in a somewhat better cause.)

The events of "There Was a Queen" occur three years after those of *Sanctuary;* the events of the published *Requiem for a Nun* are placed eight years after those of *Sanctuary.* I'd like to be able to assert that this is roughly the same chronological gap as occurs between *Sartoris* and *Sanctuary,* but Faulkner seems at times to have thought of it as an interval of six years rather than of eight.[13] In any case, the time present of *Requiem* as published is clearly contemporary with its 1951 publication date, hence something like twenty-two actual years after the 1929 dating of *Sanctuary.* (By placing the Goodwin trial six years before 1951 Faulkner could have just managed to miss World War II, and that is conceivably what he originally had in mind.) As I have already indicated, I don't wish to claim too much for the degree of integration of *Requiem* into an overall trilogy structure. Even so, it does seem reasonable to posit some kind of special relation-

ship between two texts, *Requiem* and *Sartoris,* that are both intimately related to a third text, in this instance *Sanctuary.*

Relevant here are the three surviving manuscript leaves of the
novel called *Requiem for a Nun* that Faulkner began in 1933,[14]
telling Hal Smith that it would center on a black woman and be
"a little on the esoteric side, like AS I LAY DYING." [15] That reference to *As I Lay Dying* might suggest that Faulkner expected
the work to be technically innovative in some way, but while
the three manuscript pages (actually constituting two separate
openings) are certainly written in a fairly dense prose, they
do not suggest that there were to be any particularly spectacular manipulations of point of view. One of the openings consists of a description of the Jefferson jail, a major setting both in
Sanctuary and in the 1951 *Requiem;* the other opening is set in
Gavin Stevens's office, where Stevens is interviewing a young-
ish black man and his wife about an attempt to cut the wife's
throat that had apparently been made by another black woman,
named Eunice, the previous day. There is no obvious narrative
link with the world of *Sartoris* and *Sanctuary*—except, perhaps,
that Eunice is the name of the Benbows' black cook.

On the other hand, the jail, a brief port of call for young
Bayard in *Sartoris,* had already become in *Sanctuary* an important physical and symbolic location and, what is even more to
the point, there is ample evidence in other texts to suggest that
Horace Benbow gradually "became" Gavin Stevens in Faulkner's
imagination, passing on many of his personal characteristics and
even some of his personal history—including his participation in
the trial of Lee Goodwin. As late as the 1951 *Requiem* there is at
least one instance of Gavin's voicing some thoughts about Popeye
that were once Horace's, though omitted from *Sanctuary* as published.[16] The first stage in the transition—or transmigration—
takes place during the revision of *Sanctuary,* as Faulkner strips
Horace of most of his self-conscious aestheticism and gives far
more emphasis to his well-meaning but ineffectual idealism. By
the time the three *Requiem* pages were written in December

1933 (all on the same day, incidentally), Stevens had already been created in print—first in "Smoke," published in *Harper's Monthly* for April 1932, and then in *Light in August,* published in October 1932—and Faulkner's preference for creative evolution over retrospective consistency evidently precluded the revival of a character he was finished and done with.

The projected subject-matter, plot, and themes of that 1933 *Requiem* can scarcely even be guessed at. One might think of the Nancy of "That Evening Sun" or of the way the first version of *Sanctuary* had opened with the black murderer, the best baritone in north Mississippi, singing from the jail window—but neither seems quite to fit. Given the presence of Gavin Stevens, however, and the fact that he speaks to the black couple as though they were children, there seems to be the potential for a situation akin to that in *Intruder in the Dust* or in the final chapter of *Go Down, Moses.* If, despite the shift from Benbow to Stevens, the concerns of *Sartoris* and *Sanctuary* were somehow to have been sustained, it could conceivably have been in terms of the trial of a black woman for whom the ineffectual idealist— Stevens standing in for Benbow and race now reinforcing class— would feel the reverse of that instinctive identification his predecessor had felt with Temple Drake.

Perhaps it would be wise to settle for some such term as "abortive trilogy" to describe the relationship between *Sartoris, Sanctuary,* and *Requiem.* There are certainly cross-references among them: for example, the first of the prose prologues of *Requiem* returns to that early history of Jefferson accorded so much attention in *Sartoris* and even to the figure of Colonel John Sartoris himself. It also seems feasible to think of the three novels as corresponding to that "trinity of conscience" [17] Faulkner perceived in *Moby-Dick* and sought to project in *A Fable.* Young Bayard, Horace, and Gavin would thus fall respectively into the three moral categories of knowing nothing, knowing but not caring (or not caring enough), and knowing and caring. If that suggests an unduly positive evaluation of Gavin Stevens it is necessary to remember that Faulkner's moral activists, including the battalion runner in *A Fable* itself, are almost always precipitators of disaster. But there is no evidence that Faulkner was thinking in such terms as early as *Sartoris* or *Sanctuary* (though he had certainly read *Moby-Dick* by then), and one could not in any case argue that the series is closed by the 1951 *Requiem* either as specifically or as elegantly as the Snopes trilogy is concluded by *The Mansion*, which not only alternates essentially *Hamlet* material with essentially *Town* material but also shifts technically between the points of view used in the two earlier novels.

There is, of course, a profound difference between a planned trilogy, as I take "Snopes" to have been, and the kind of gradually evolved or (less politely) ad hoc trilogy into which I have tried to fit *Sartoris, Sanctuary,* and *Requiem.* But I see no reason to be deterred from perceiving—or projecting—relationships among works in the Faulkner canon simply because Faulkner himself invoked the term "trilogy" on only the one occasion. Indeed, I think it can and should be asked whether there may not exist additional pairings, trilogies, abortive trilogies, linked stories, or other significant groupings of ostensibly discrete texts. And if so, how are we to read such interconnected fictions? Does Faulkner allow himself to assume that the reader of novel B will already have read novel A, or quite the reverse? Does he reward the reader who is extensively familiar with his work over and above the reader who is not?

Once such questions are asked, it is immediately clear that there are several instances of novels and stories standing in particularly close or suggestive relationships to each other. Carvel Collins taught us many years ago to think in terms of a "pairing" of *The Sound and the Fury* and *As I Lay Dying,* and I have myself suggested that they might jointly be linked with *Absalom, Absalom!* as a kind of trilogy on the multivalence of truth.[18] The stories in *Knight's Gambit,* to choose a very different example, somehow demand to be linked, through Gavin Stevens, to that more extended "detective" fiction *Intruder in the Dust*—which itself seems clearly to refer back to and comment upon the final segment of *Go Down, Moses*. *Big Woods*, simply by existing as a work in the Faulkner canon, also offers an implicit comment upon *Go Down, Moses* as a whole, and there is perhaps something yet to be better understood about the relationship between *Absalom* and *Pylon*, the novel Faulkner wrote when he ran into difficulties with the more ambitious undertaking. There are arguably elements common to *Pylon* and to Faulkner's other New Orleans novels, *Mosquitoes* and *The Wild Palms* (they all deal, for example, with varieties of permanent or temporary deracination), and there can be no doubt that some of the finest short stories are narrative or emotional spin-offs from the creative surges that generated major novels—that "Barn Burning" is intimately related to *The Hamlet* (of which it once formed the opening chapter), "That Evening Sun" to *The Sound and the Fury*, and "Dry September" to *Light in August*.

Clearly, Faulkner's texts may fall into patterns of relationship that simply cannot be accommodated by such conventional terms as trilogy, tetralogy, and so on. The many appearances of Gavin Stevens present just such a problem—especially if he is given retroactive credit (or discredit) for the activities of his secret sharer Horace Benbow—and in making out my case for a *Sartoris/Sanctuary/Requiem* trilogy I conveniently left out of account not only *The Unvanquished*, which fills in so much of the early background to *Sartoris*, but also *The Reivers*, which returns to the world of Miss Reba's even more directly than does *Requiem* itself. Interestingly enough, *The Reivers* is set at a point in time roughly a decade earlier than the time present of *Sartoris*, thus offering the possibility of grouping together *The Reivers, Sartoris, Sanctuary*, and *Requiem* as a more or less regularly spaced chronicle of Jefferson's middle class—with *The Unvanquished* as a rather more distant historical complement. Or perhaps the central sequence runs through *The Reivers, Sanctuary*, and *Requiem*—Faulkner's Memphis or cathouse trilogy, richly commented upon by the semifictional "Mississippi" essay and by the fact that Faulkner, who once said that the best job ever offered him was that of landlord of a brothel,[19] evidently identified with Mr. Binford.

Even the Snopes trilogy itself is by no means entirely self-contained: I suspect that it may be the favorable impression of Charles Mallison created by *Intruder in the Dust* that enables readers to be more patient with him in *The Town* and *The Mansion* than his somewhat abrasive language and attitudes might otherwise permit. Similarly—though I am conscious of venturing into dangerous waters here—there seems little doubt that we carry over into *Absalom, Absalom!* a good deal of what we have learned of Quentin and of Mr. Compson from our reading of *The Sound and the Fury*. The danger, indeed, is that we may carry over a little too much: I'm not at all sure, for example, that the temptation to import the "incest motif" from *The Sound and the Fury* isn't another of the multiple false leads in *Absalom*, another of the ways in which Faulkner delays our seeing what ought to have been obvious or at any rate guessable enough from the start. What Quentin and Shreve imagine Sutpen saying to Henry— "*So it's the miscegenation, not the incest, which you cant bear*" [20]— may, within *Absalom*, be no less applicable to Quentin himself, and there seems no compelling reason to consider the novel as anything other than a self-sufficient text, although one left deliberately open to different readings by different readers who bring to it different qualifications—including differing degrees of exposure to other Faulknerian texts. Indeed, it is no part of my argument to suggest that any of the novels and stories are individually diminished by their interplay with other texts, deprived of their uniqueness, independence, or self-sufficiency, or rendered any less capable of being read and contemplated in isolation. Even in his one acknowledged trilogy Faulkner quite often reintroduces characters and situations in terms that subtly modify them to suit the purposes of that particular text: hence, for example, the differing accounts of Mink's murder of Houston and his subsequent expectation of assistance from Flem.

The existence of recurring characters and of the whole Yokna-patawphan apparatus nevertheless encourages the reader of a particular work to bring to bear upon it the experience gained from reading other Faulkner works. At one level, of course, the process is not unlike that involved in the recognition of any literary allusion, except that in Faulkner what is to be gained from the other text or texts includes not only a familiarity with particular characters and locations (the Old Frenchman place, after all, is as vital a linking device as any of Faulkner's human figures) but also a progressive awareness of how a Faulkner text is to be approached, engaged, and ultimately possessed (grappled, boarded, and seized I had almost said, remembering those curious nautical allusions in *Sanctuary*). Faulkner, that is to say, gradually teaches his audience how to read him, and while such an assertion could no doubt be made of many innovative novelists, there is an unusual deliberateness to his method of drawing attention to available clarifications of whatever difficulty is currently being encountered.

Despite the power of the Yoknapatawphan idea—despite, too, the limitations implicit in the chronological sequence of Faulkner's published work—it certainly remains possible for the Faulknerian fictions to be collectively viewed in terms of infinitely variable patterns of interrelationships and subjected to kaleidoscopic shifts of perspective untrammelled by the inconvenient scruples of textual and biographical scholarship. There can be no doubt, as I argued earlier, that Faulkner did from an early stage project large-scale creative undertakings on into the future—that his imagination was entirely capable of ranging forward in both general and specific terms over works he had not yet begun to write—and to think of Yoknapatawpha as a vast imaginative conception Faulkner only fragmentarily realized on paper is in effect to acknowledge the possibility that a given text may contain not only the obvious references backward but also deliberate references forward. For my own part, however, I must confess to never having found it very helpful to think of *Absalom* as implicitly fitted into the temporal framework of *The Sound and the Fury*, to try to feed into Quentin's act of suicide the supplemental motivation that might be reckoned to flow from his recent exposure to the final stages of the Sutpen tragedy. I prefer the coldly practical explanation that, having decided to use Quentin in *Absalom*, Faulkner in order to avoid absurdity had no choice but to place the Harvard portions within Quentin's lifetime as already publicly established. Premonitions of *Absalom*, in short, are simply not there for me in *The Sound and the Fury*, even though the earlier novel cannot help but be a tangible presence on the sidelines of the later.

The Unvanquished, on the other hand, is a complexly referential text. Retrospectively, it expands upon and modifies the Civil War narratives earlier incorporated into *Sartoris*, provides a radically new perspective upon the treatment in *Light in August* of the deaths of the two abolitionists, Miss Burden's father and brother, and offers an extraordinarily concise and cogent summary of the character of Thomas Sutpen as revealed in *Absalom*, its immediate predecessor. But it also can be said to create prospectively, in advance of their far more significant roles in *Go Down, Moses*, the figures of Uncles Buck and Buddy McCaslin. Other novels yield instances of what might be called negative anticipation: the limited characterization of Eula Varner in *The Hamlet*, for example, was perhaps determined by Faulkner's already formulated intentions for *The Town*, even as aspects of Narcissa Benbow's character seem to have been held back in *Sartoris* for subsequent release in *Sanctuary* and "There Was a Queen." It's even possible that the obviously incomplete presentation of the trial scene in *Sanctuary* was related to an expectation on Faulkner's part that he would return to it in a later novel.

We are familiar with the proposition, most famously articulated by T. S. Eliot, that each new work of art modifies all of its predecessors, and there is undoubtedly a sense in which each individual work of any writer modifies, conditions our response to, every other work by that same writer. Our reading of *Typee* is affected by our awareness of Melville as the author of *Moby-Dick;* even our reading of *Moby-Dick* at some level takes into account the existence of *Typee.* But Faulkner's deliberate use of recurrent characters, locations, and situations seems a way of insisting that in reading any one of his novels we take consciously into account, first, a set of specifically linked novels and stories and, secondly—at any rate, potentially—the entire corpus of his published work. The public face, so to speak, of this design is the pseudogeographical system that Faulkner called Yoknapatawpha County, and yet the kind of interaction between separate texts to which I'm now referring goes beyond the limits of what Yoknapatawpha can reasonably be held to represent. What simultaneously separates and unites such novels as *The Unvanquished* and *Sartoris,* or *Sanctuary* and *The Reivers,* or indeed *The Sound and the Fury* and *Absalom, Absalom!* is something analogous to what occurs *within* so many of the novels—a shift of perspective, a change in narrative point of view, the presentation of a different facet of human experience, which obliges us to modify our initial assumptions about a character, a situation, or a set of attitudes and beliefs.

Faulkner seems characteristically to have found his resolutions not precisely in irresolution but in the recognition of alternatives, of opposing truths, rather in the manner of that Book of the Grotesque, the opening section of Sherwood Anderson's *Winesburg, Ohio,* which was so important to his early self-realization as an artist. I spoke earlier of Faulkner's fiction as constituting "a Doomsday Book" of the regional imagination, "a vast compendium of narrated tales and lives, of legends and speaking fables." An alternative way of contemplating his work as a whole—indeed, of seeing all the texts on a single plane, in time as well as in space—might be to think of each novel, and even each story, as a separate chapter in a Faulknerian Book of the Grotesque, an independent fable of human experience ("the old verities and truths of the heart")[21] that nonetheless reveals its full meaning and implications only when read in the context of all the others. In a curious way *The Wild Palms*, which has so often seemed to lie outside the Faulknerian mainstream, has a special claim to be considered the paradigmatic Faulknerian text, founded more absolutely than any other upon that juxtaposition of discontinuous, contradictory, and yet in some sense complementary narratives that is recognizable as the fundamental principle running throughout the whole of Faulkner's infinitely rich and various life's work. *Sartoris, Sanctuary,* and *Requiem for a Nun* may not constitute an ideal or even a conventional trilogy, but—like the double narrative of *The Wild Palms* and the story-chapters of *Go Down, Moses,* like *The Sound and the Fury* and *Absalom, Absalom!,* like the entire Faulknerian corpus—they certainly meet the criterion, profoundly if somewhat enigmatically invoked by Faulkner himself, of being "contrapuntal in integration." [22]

William Faulkner: The Two Voices

The two voices of my title take their origin from Tennyson's poem "The Two Voices"—essentially a dialogue between despair and hope, suicide and rebirth, negative and positive thinking, resolved in favor of the latter but in terms that leave one wondering whether the defeated, nay-saying voice might not after all have had the better of the argument. In truth, however, the title need not have "come from" anywhere. It is simply a way of insisting upon the pervasiveness of dialogue, debate, and opposition throughout William Faulkner's work, and at the same time of avoiding a term like "dialectical," with which Faulkner himself would probably have been uneasy, and that suggests in any case a far higher degree of ultimate definition and resolution than most Faulknerian texts either achieve or even pursue.

There is, of course, nothing new in insisting upon Faulkner's characteristic counterpointing of characters, themes, and structural units. In the late 1950s Walter J. Slatoff wrote very perceptively about what he called Faulkner's "polar imagination," his fondness for antithesis and conflict, his frequent ambiguity, his often oxymoronic and densely negative style—as when Hightower, in *Light in August*, compares reading Tennyson to "listening in a cathedral to a eunuch chanting in a language which he does not even need to not understand"[1]—and his apparent determination to frustrate the reader's lust for resolutions. Slatoff seemed in the end to become frustrated by precisely those habits of Faulkner's mind he had so interestingly illuminated, taking the too extravagant position that the "polar imagination" was almost schizophrenic in its intensity, ultimately allied itself with disorder, and reflected "a deliberate quest for failure" on Faulkner's part.[2] It seems to me unquestionable that Faulkner's imagination does indeed tend toward polarization—toward patterns of duality and even multiplicity in his structures, in his demography (by which I mean the configurations of characters within particular texts), and in his handling of questions of moral judgment. I tend, however, to see that sort of patterning as conscious and controlled rather than simply obsessive (or schizoid). And I would argue that it operated for Faulkner as a kind of exploratory device, directed toward the expression or— better, perhaps—the exposition of complexities that he believed to be inherent in his own experience as a human being who happened to inhabit a particular place at a particular moment in time.

It is in the first place sufficiently clear that Faulkner's novels are characteristically "open" in ways that go beyond the typical open-ended novel of the late nineteenth or early twentieth centuries—*The Portrait of a Lady*, for example, or *The Ambassadors*, or *Lord Jim*. At the conclusion of such novels, typically focused upon some central figure, the reader is invited, or incited, to arrive at a quasi-independent judgment of that figure's actions in the presented past or to speculate as to his or her probable conduct in the unnarrated future. Faulkner's novels are never so narrowly focused; if they seem to be so, that appearance proves on closer inspection to be illusory. *Soldiers' Pay*, untypical in many things, is thoroughly typical insofar as it introduces, and sets off against each other, a whole range of characters from different social backgrounds; it also possesses, in Donald Mahon, an ostensibly central figure who is effectively not there. In *Sartoris (Flags in the Dust)* the primary contrast between the hard self-destructiveness of young Bayard and the soft but scarcely less wilful dissolution of Horace Benbow is blurred not so much by the failure of those two characters ever to meet (many of Faulkner's dialogues are carried on between people who never encounter each other in person) as by the proliferation of supplementary oppositions between Miss Jenny and Narcissa, between young Bayard and his dead brother John, between several family groups—Sartorises, Benbows, Mitchells, MacCallums, and the two black families—and even between different generations of the same family, between the living and the dead. Though *The Sound and the Fury* and *As I Lay Dying* attain much greater structural coherence, they again deploy a generous range of characters, and these are often disposed in pairs, or even triples, as embodiments of different psychological traits or philosophical positions—sometimes, as Judith Wittenberg has suggested, as autobiographical projections of different facets of Faulkner's own psyche.[5] It would be hard to get a random group of critics to agree upon a candidate for the role of hero in either novel, and if Caddy and Addie can perhaps be claimed as heroines, it is only in a very special sense: like Donald Mahon—like the two John Sartorises of *Flags in the Dust*—neither of them is truly present, and their respective novels revolve precisely upon that absence.

Many of Faulkner's texts are "open" almost in the sense in which one speaks of an open forum or an open debate. They are town meetings of the imagination, loud with the rhetoric of advocacy, complaint, and self-justification. In *The Sound and the Fury* and *As I Lay Dying* the air is full of voices, speaking (it is part of their tragedy) to the reader rather than to each other. *Absalom, Absalom!*, too, is almost deafeningly full of conflicting voices. The clear patterns of opposition between Miss Rosa and Mr. Compson as initial narrators and between Quentin and Shreve as narrative partners simultaneously cut across and interpenetrate the central non-confrontation between Sutpen and Charles Bon and the overarching opposition between Sutpen and Quentin, the man of obsessive action and the boy of self-perpetuated immaturity, the two figures upon whose polarity the central tension of the novel depends—between whom, so to speak, it is stretched taut.

Even in novels in which the sense of active altercation is less pronounced, the patterns of opposition and contrast still persist. Many such patterns, large and small, are identified in Thomas L. McHaney's excellent study of *The Wild Palms*, and it is immediately clear, especially in a work Faulkner himself described as contrapuntal, that Harry Wilbourne is set off against the tall convict, Charlotte against the pregnant woman of "Old Man," and the two narratives one against the other. *Light in August* depends absolutely on the constant interplay among Lena Grove, Joe Christmas, and Gail Hightower but also on the implicit cross-references between Lena and Miss Burden, between Joe Christmas and Percy Grimm, between Byron Bunch and Lucas Burch, and so on. It is a critical commonplace that *The Hamlet* is given unity by the multiplicity of those crisscrossing contrasts and pairings of character and theme that bind it together as one laces up a shoe. And by the time he wrote *Go Down, Moses,* Faulkner was ready to integrate a whole series of apparently distinct oppositions within a single contrapuntal structure, pivoting the whole network of cross-references upon the fourth section of "The Bear" and specifically on that debate in the commissary between Ike McCaslin on the one hand and his cousin Cass Edmonds on the other.

From that point onward the debate becomes a standard element in almost all of Faulkner's novels. One thinks of the long discussions between Gavin Stevens and Charles Mallison in *Intruder in the Dust;* the play-within-a-novel and inquisition-within-a-play of *Requiem for a Nun;* the set-piece confrontation between the Marshal and the Corporal in *A Fable;* the unspoken dialogue among the three narrators of *The Town;* the repetition of that technique in the middle section of *The Mansion*, supplemented by another implicit dialogue among the three sections themselves, entitled "Mink," "Linda," and "Flem." In *The Reivers* there is even the ghostly presence of the figures of Virtue and Non-virtue, hovering around the vulnerable innocence of the young hero like the Good and Bad Angels in *Dr. Faustus*. Nor is that a farfetched comparison, least of all when the hero is called Lucius Priest. In Faulkner, and especially in the later Faulkner, we seem at times to be witnessing a kind of morality play—or even a sequence of morality plays. Reading *The Wild Palms* is rather like watching a pair of medieval pageant-wagons circling around, presenting in turn the successive stages of their sometimes comic, sometimes tragic, always purposive dramas, one from the Old Testament, the other, dense with parallelism, from the New. (In *As I Lay Dying* we are now on the wagon itself, now watching with the audience—none of whom seem anxious to occupy the front rows.) *A Fable*, self-categorized by its title, is only the most obvious and elaborate expression of a tendency toward moral fable that is arguably latent as far back as *Soldiers' Pay*, or even *Marionettes* and *The Marble Faun*.

One might add, since it is integral to Faulkner's fondness for seeing things from plural viewpoints, that most of his characters do turn out to be supplied with both categories of angel. The multiplication of characters, of contrasts, and of potentially available points of view provides a perspective within which the reader is eventually obliged to concede the possibility of making out some sort of sympathetic case for even the most deplorable of Faulkner's failures and villains—for Anse Bundren, for example, and even Jason Compson. The final chapter of *Sanctuary* extorts, in however equivocal a fashion, a flicker of sympathy for the hitherto loathsome Popeye, and Flem Snopes, already pitied for his impotence, has a moment of dignity at the conclusion of *The Mansion*. A similar process of gradual, grudging revaluation is enacted within the text of the novels on those occasions when the initial impression of a character subsequently proves to be radically inadequate. Joe Christmas is very much a case in point, and in *Intruder in the Dust* we eventually arrive with Charles Mallison at a deeper and more sympathetic understanding of Lucas Beauchamp, and even of Old Man Gowrie. Alternatively, an otherwise admirable figure may in due course reveal limitations and flaws; Ratliff in *The Hamlet*, for example. And in some cases—most notably those of Ike McCaslin and Gavin Stevens—the reader is constantly swung pendulumlike between approval and disapproval, sympathy and rejection, until coming finally to rest in the realization that judgment in such instances, perhaps in most Faulknerian instances, may be a matter not of "either/or" but rather of "both/and."

Faulkner's texts, in fact, are not only extraordinarily open, they are also unusually fluid. The moral judgments extorted from the reader by the very need to respond to the actions in which some of the characters engage (burning barns, murdering middle-aged spinsters, depriving idiots of their favorite cows) are always provisional, pending the next twist of the narrative, the next shift in point of view. Characterization itself is never fixed and finite but always in process, obliging the reader to engage in continual readjustments. It is for such reasons that the episode of the Old Frenchman place and the salted gold hoard is placed at the very end of *The Hamlet*, when the reader has long become comfortable with Ratliff, and Ratliff with himself. Neither remembers until too late the cautionary tale, the hubristic fable, of Ab Snopes and the cream separator Ratliff had himself told earlier in the novel. What Ratliff discovers is that Flem Snopes is the Pat Stamper of the Yoknapatawphan real estate market. What the reader is reassured to learn, as the judgmental pendulum again swings back a little, is that if Ratliff is capable of the gullibility of the unsoured Ab he also possesses the same rueful humor: his "We even got a new place to dig" corresponds precisely to Ab's comment, as his wife puts the same gallon of milk through the separator for the umpteenth time, "It looks like she is fixing to get a heap of pleasure and satisfaction outen it." [4]

One of the most remarkable instances of the provisionality of characterization in Faulkner is that provided by the successive appearances of Mink Snopes in *The Hamlet, The Town,* and *The Mansion,* and it seems useful, if mildly digressive, to make the point that in this respect, as in so many others, Faulkner's late fiction neither "betrays" his earlier work nor significantly diverges from it. It unfortunately remains a widely held view that Faulkner's creative arteries hardened in his, and the century's, fifties, and that he then abandoned the complexities and ambiguities of his early and middle periods in favor of a more or less coherent world view, roughly coincident with that of Gavin Stevens and consisting largely of the resounding affirmation, and tedious reaffirmation, of unimpeachable moral platitudes. Grossly misunderstood by many of his first critics, Faulkner doubtless sought in some of his later fiction to clarify, to spell out, what in his earlier novels had been deemed obscure. But spelling out often meant, for Faulkner, an intensification rather than an abandonment of previous techniques, and the real substance of his saying did not in any case undergo significant change.

There is no obvious discrepancy between the Nobel Prize speech of 1950 and Faulkner's private comment to Warren Beck in 1941 that he had been "writing all the time about honor, truth, pity, consideration, the capacity to endure well grief and misfortune and injustice and then endure again."[5] No Faulkner novel probes the problems of moral responsibility, the ambiguities of intention and act, more acutely and painfully than does *Requiem for a Nun,* published in 1951. Nor, as Noel Polk's study everywhere makes clear,[6] is any Faulkner novel more openended. If we persist in misinterpreting, or in failing to interpret, *A Fable,* that is perhaps because of our determination to extract a philosophy—coherent, unitary, definable—from what seems so self-evidently philosophical a work. But Thomas Hardy, another novelist often accused of having a philosophy, always insisted that what he offered was nothing other than "a series of seemings,"[7] a set of fragmentary impressions of life and truth as they might appear to different people at different moments. And the issues raised in *A Fable,* although given an unusually elaborate development, are finally surrendered to the reader in much the same unresolved state as those presented at the end of *The Sound and the Fury, Light in August, Go Down, Moses,* and all the rest.

The familiar patterns of opposition and contrast still prevail in *A Fable;* they have simply become more self-conscious and more systematic. The old verities of the Nobel Prize speech are indeed dramatized, but the faith that Faulkner sought to keep with mankind, and in mankind, was grounded, as the Nobel Prize speech itself makes clear, in an unblinking recognition of man's capacity and indeed aptitude for every species of inhumanity and folly. It was not that Faulkner wanted it both ways—he saw that it *was* both ways, or indeed, a multiplicity of ways. His fictional world, crowded with echoing forensic voices, with paired characters, with equivocal heroes and emasculated villains, with contrapuntal structures, unresolved meanings, and withheld judgments, is from first to last the embodiment of that vision, the enactment of what he called in the Nobel Prize speech "the problems of the human heart in conflict with itself." [8]

Although the materials and settings of Faulkner's fictional world, are, of course, almost exclusively southern, it would clearly be a gross oversimplification to argue that his characteristic habits of mind—or habits of imagination—were themselves directly attributable to his having sprung from and grown up in that extraordinary mass of social, historical, and political contradictions called the South. At the same time, many of the features of his fiction that I have just been discussing can certainly be associated with the necessary self-consciousness of the regional writer, especially of the regional writer who is aware, as Faulkner undoubtedly was, of the strategies, at once richly traditional and perennially vital, of pastoral literature. The sheer density of minor characters in such early novels as *Soldiers' Pay* and *Flags in the Dust* clearly has much to do with the regionalist's need to map his region, establish its particularity, create a world at once purposively symbolic and yet sufficiently populated and land-scaped to command the willing credulity of his potential urban readers, to whom the region will specifically, and almost by defi-nition, be unfamiliar. (Even *Wuthering Heights,* which some-times gets taught and discussed as though it were a hermetically sealed experiment in technique, covers a remarkably wide socio-logical range.) The multiplicity of contrasted figures and con-tending voices arises from that same regional self-consciousness and in particular from the almost inevitable impulse to chal-lenge the standard regional stereotypes. As Hardy deliberately rejected the conventional Victorian identification of rural labor-ers with a stolid, dim-witted, monolithic figure called Hodge, so Faulkner, as Cleanth Brooks has shown,[9] set out with similar de-liberateness to display to the nonsouthern world the rich inner variety of the class of people known collectively as "poor whites."

Faulkner's readiness to temper the presentation of heroes and villains alike may itself have something to do with the regional-ist-pastoralist's concern, on the one hand, to avoid paragons of virtue who might seem implausible to his sophisticated urban readership and, on the other, to defend his region against those same sophisticates and their all-too-ready contempt and dis-missal. Those who travel overseas become familiar with the ex-perience of defending abroad the policies of governments to which they are, at home, utterly and actively opposed, and the regionalist-pastoralist is no less ambiguously engaged in "rep-resenting" his region in distant places—as Faulkner's fellow townspeople half understood when they complained, as they of-ten did, of his "misrepresentin' Mississippi." He (the pastoralist) is also necessarily engaged in setting off his region against the dominant culture of the court, or of modern urban-industrial so-ciety, and for Faulkner, as a southerner, the sense of that distinc-tiveness was peculiarly and painfully acute. He was a member, nationally speaking, not merely of a minority culture but of a re-jected culture, a culture that had in one sense been given shape and coherence by the very experience of military and political defeat and that continued to be sustained by its difference from, and opposition to, a dominant culture that was itself too secure in its dominance to concern itself overmuch with anxieties about its own identity.

Often, as one might expect, it is almost impossible to distinguish confidently between what Faulkner owes to his native southernness and what to his adopted pastoralism. The use of the set debate, for example, can be associated with the traditional dialogues of pastoral poetry (including such modern versions as those of Robert Frost), but the prevailing tone and temper of the altercations that recur throughout Faulkner's fiction would also seem to owe a good deal to the conventions of southern oratory. Faulkner himself, in an excessively self-critical mood, told Malcolm Cowley that his style was the result of the experience of writing in solitude together with the complicating factor of "an inherited regional or geographical (Hawthorne would say, racial) curse. You might say, studbook style: 'by Southern Rhetoric out of Solitude' or 'Oratory out of Solitude.'" [10] However that may be, one can perhaps suggest that those factors—historical, political, social, cultural, and economic—that for so long kept the South depressed, and kept it solid, also lent a peculiar intensity and vigor to Faulkner's personal sense of regional identification, hence to the expression of that identification in his work. I suggest, indeed, that it was just this intensity and vigor which informed the extraordinary amplitude of his regional creation and the extraordinary ambitiousness of his exploitation of basic pastoral strategies. It appears, that is to say, to have been a more complex fate to be a Mississippian than either a Vermonter like Frost or a Dorset man like Hardy. Yeats's literary and personal relationship with his native Ireland perhaps offers a closer comparison, as Brooks has suggested,[11] although one somewhat undercut by Yeats's having been a much less consistent and systematic pastoralist.

The difference between writers like Hardy and Frost on the one hand and Faulkner and Yeats on the other I take to be essentially political. For both Hardy and Faulkner, the region is ultimately their material rather than their subject; they speak primarily to nonregional audiences and draw upon regional material as a means of achieving dramatized expression of fundamental human themes and values. But for Hardy, as for Frost, what is distinctively regional belongs already to the past; the old ways and the old speech are dead or dying; the region, as a region, has no real future. So Hardy writes again and again of the lost world of his own childhood. Faulkner, on the other hand, insists (as does Yeats) upon the necessary preservation into a foreseeable future of a regional distinctiveness that remains, in his own day, a cultural and political reality. Though deeply and painfully aware of the erosion of values and customs, and of the destruction of the environment, Faulkner harks back to the past chiefly in order to bring it contrastively to bear upon the regional present (in *Absalom, Absalom!*, for example, or in *Go Down, Moses*). The resulting dialogue between past and present may indeed serve to demonstrate to his (relatively few) southern readers the need to keep in touch with regional roots and to move forward to a regional future built upon acceptance of the best features of the past and rejection of the worst. But it is at the same time a technique for providing his (relatively numerous) nonsouthern, nonrural readers with a multidimensioned presentation of a particular regional society and culture and for drawing attention—through the implicit dialogue between past and present, supplemented by explicit debates between such characters as Ike and Cass—to precisely those basic values, surviving or eroding, which his whole regionalist-pastoralist strategy is designed to assert and affirm.

When I was discussing earlier some of the formal features characteristically found in Faulkner's novels—a profusion of oppositions, a lack of heroes and heroines, a tendency toward openness and final irresolution—it must have seemed that such generalizations had little application to *The Reivers*, that apparently unintentional but nonetheless felicitous conclusion to Faulkner's

career. *The Reivers,* after all, projects not only a clear moral resolution and a resoundingly victorious hero but also a kind of
geniality and even serenity that sorts oddly with the anguish
of so many of the earlier works, including those specifically recalled within *The Reivers* itself. No doubt increasing age and
crowding honors had encouraged Faulkner to look back upon
his own handiwork and see that it was good. He may even have
felt that he had, in Lawrence's phrase, come through, in creative
and even in personal terms. It seems significant, however, that
The Reivers, though so distinctively Yoknapatawphan and autobiographical, should have been written in Charlottesville, Virginia—the South still, of course, but a very different South,
older, wealthier, more self-assured, closer (geographically and
politically) to the centers of national power, already more at ease
with, because less affected by, the changes beginning to sweep
over the region as a whole. In the 1950s Faulkner's travels to various parts of the world had strengthened his belief that devotion
to locality and region must at some level be subsumed into patriotism, and patriotism in its turn into a kind of internationalism.
The speech he gave to the Southern Historical Association meeting in November 1955 [12] made absolutely clear his sense of the
need for a progressively more expansive and inclusive human
commitment, and by the time he wrote *The Reivers* he seems to
have grown altogether more at ease with his matured, if still
complex and even ambiguous, view of the world, and corre-
spondingly less exercised about his specifically regional loyalties.

But *The Reivers* is of course a moral fable, just as surely as *A
Fable* itself. It is possible to argue, indeed, that Faulkner's old
habits of opposition and alternation persisted to the last, and that
The Reivers is properly read as the particular fable—simple,
positive, serene—that we are invited to set off against the dark
complexities of *A Fable,* that novel full of slaughter and of sui-
cides. There is a sense, that is to say, in which the opposition of *A
Fable* and *The Reivers* represents the dialogue of Tennyson's
"The Two Voices" writ large. So seen, *The Reivers* falls into

place not as Faulkner's deliberately final word, but as one work among many, expressive of truths, but not of *the* truth. An authentic and indispensable Faulknerian voice, but not the only Faulknerian voice—merely (by which I mean magnificently) another intervention in that long unresolved because irresolvable dialogue of one human heart in conflict with itself, and secondarily with its region, that we know as the Faulkner canon.

Faulkner's Masters

The late Richard P. Adams published in 1962 a long and extremely important essay, "The Apprenticeship of William Faulkner," [1] in which he provided substantial and extensive documentation for the view that Faulkner's career as a novelist was based upon "an enormous amount of reading, intelligently chosen from the best literature available in Western civilization." That view was by no means universally or even widely held at the time when Adams wrote, and even today there are too many critics who seem not to have absorbed the wisdom of the essay's second paragraph:

> It is true that Faulkner was provincial, and that in some ways the province in which he was born and reared and educated, and lived almost the whole of his life, is one of the less civilized parts of the Western world. But to conclude from these premises, as some appear to have done, that Faulkner was culturally isolated, that he was an ignorant genius, born in a manger, miraculously visited by the muses, and receiving inspiration for masterpiece after masterpiece out of the air without any teaching or learning, is to be guilty of incredible nonsense. There can be no

royal road to the kind of work Faulkner did between 1928 and 1942. Certainly the man who could do it was a genius, but not even he could have done it without the hardest kind of study, thought, and labor. What came out of him in those fertile years had to come in part from an enormous amount of written matter previously absorbed into him. Granted he was provincial. But he was also a highly sophisticated young man, who, living far from the capital, could not take his culture for granted but had to sweat for it, and who succeeded in educating himself more thoroughly, and in some ways more systematically, than most college graduates are educated.[2]

In the years since Adams's pioneering article, much additional evidence of Faulkner's copious and diverse reading has been brought to the attention of scholars. My purpose here is not so much to supplement that evidence—though I may do so in minor ways—as to look back over the ground thus far covered and attempt to discriminate between those writers who "influenced" Faulkner in specific, directly identifiable ways, and those whose importance for him was at once more general and more pervasive—the masters, in short, to whom his apprenticeship was served.

Since the contents of the Rowanoak bookshelves at the time of Faulkner's death[3] provide so inadequate an indication of his early reading, it is necessary to rely a good deal on other sources of information and especially upon Faulkner's own statements in interviews. Unfortunately, but perhaps understandably, such statements are often suspect, not just because their tone and content depended so much on Faulkner's reaction to his interviewers, or because he believed that evasiveness was perfectly justifiable as a defense of his privacy, but also because he developed over the years a series of formulaic answers to the questions most frequently asked. Statistically prominent among these was a standard inquiry about his reading, and students of Faulkner have long been familiar with the general shape of the standard reply, which had already been evolved by the time of the Nagano seminars in 1955: "I read *Don Quixote* usually once every year. I read *Moby Dick* every four or five years. I read *Madame Bovary, The Brothers Karamazov*. I read the Old Testament, oh, once every ten or fifteen years. I have a complete Shakespeare in one volume that I carry with me and I read a little of that almost any time. I read in and out of Dickens some every year, and in and out of Conrad, the same way, some every year."[4] There were, of course, minor variations from time to time: one of the regular names might drop out on a particular occasion, a less familiar one slip in. But the central group of titles and names remained consistent: *Don Quixote* and *Moby-Dick* always; *Madame Bovary* and *The Brothers Karamazov* almost always; Shakespeare, invariably in that single portable volume; Balzac, Dickens, and Conrad, usually without specification of particular works.

Archaeological exploration of earlier Faulkner interviews makes it possible to trace back the origins of this particular formula to 1931 and a list composed exclusively of *Moby-Dick* and *The Nigger of the "Narcissus":* in one interview of that year Faulkner named these as his favorite books, in another he explained that he would "just like to have written those two books more than any others I can think of."[5] Clearly Faulkner was not acknowledging "influences," as that term is customarily understood, but offering—as an author newly confident of his own powers—a salute to his literary ancestors, identifying what were for him the pinnacles of achievement in the art to which he had dedicated himself, proclaiming the touchstones by which he intended to judge his own work and that of his contemporaries. Faulkner himself made the point very firmly at Nagano, in responding to a question as to why he had not included Joyce and Proust in the reading—or rather rereading—list already quoted:

The names I mentioned yesterday were the names of the men who I think influenced me. When I read Joyce and Proust it is possible that my career as a writer was already fixed, so that there was no chance for it to be influenced other than in the tricks of the trade, you might say, but I think the bad [habits] had been established. When I named the writers that I'd read, I did not mean by that that I had not read anything else and did not read anything else, but they were the ones that, to me, had been masters, and I felt towards them the same loyalty and affection and respect the young student feels towards his professor, his master, which doesn't mean that the young student doesn't exchange ideas with his contemporaries. Joyce was, well, in a way, a contemporary of mine; Proust, almost a contemporary of mine, that is, he was writing towards the top of his talent at the time when I was writing towards mine.[6]

The essential distinction Faulkner makes here is between the "masters," those who influenced him in the broadest and deepest sense, by guiding and inciting him to the pursuit of his own kind of excellence, and the "contemporaries," those great writers of his own time whom he read at a later stage in his career, when he was susceptible only to influences of a narrower and shallower sort—what he calls "tricks of the trade." The generalization is sweeping and doubtless in need of qualification, but it remains Faulkner's own perception and, as such, fundamental to any attempt to make sense not only of his densely crowded literary background—the product of his voracious reading as a youth and young man—but also of his readiness, as an artist, to absorb from the work of other writers whatever he thought would be advantageous to his own. In the 1920s, as Martin Kreiswirth has shown,[7] Faulkner engaged in the deliberate reworking of existing poems, not as an act of plagiarism but as a conscious literary exercise; once launched upon his career as a novelist he was launched equally upon that career of constant thievery he believed to be inseparable from his vocation: "A writer," he said at Nagano, "is completely rapacious, he has no morals whatever, he will steal from any source."[8]

It is evidently in some such terms that Faulkner's polite reference to the "exchange" of ideas with his contemporaries is to be understood, and the most readily identifiable "influences" upon his novels are indeed those of other twentieth-century novelists—especially in those years leading up to *The Sound and the Fury* when he was searching almost desperately (so the evidence of *Mosquitoes* would suggest) for a usable contemporary idiom. "The two great men in my time were Mann and Joyce," Faulkner declared in 1955,[9] and both names appear frequently in his recorded interviews. *Buddenbrooks*, the Mann work he most often mentions by name, was first published in translation in the United States in 1924, and it is tempting to think that it contributed to the working out not only of *Flags in the Dust*, his novel about the decline of the Sartoris family, but also of his very different novel about the decline of the Compson family. Although there are few direct correspondences between Mann's characters and Faulkner's, many ingredients in the situation of the Buddenbrooks family recur in *The Sound and the Fury* and in both novels it is above all the failure of humanity, the denial of love, that destroys both the family and its individual members.

Many of Faulkner's numerous debts to Joyce have already been pointed out—notably by Adams, whose suggestion that Faulkner read portions of *Ulysses* as they appeared in the *Little Review* has gained support from subsequently published Faulkner letters[10]—and many more no doubt remain to be identified. It seems entirely possible, for example, that the effects of simultaneity striven for in *Soldiers' Pay* owe something to the "Wandering Rocks" section of *Ulysses*, and that Elmer's distressful sacrifice of his painting at a critical moment in the unpublished "Portrait of Elmer Hodge" derives from Faulkner's recollection of the use to which Leopold Bloom had been obliged to put the prize story from *Titbits*. These are indeed "tricks of the trade," however, and even at this level Faulkner, for all his admiration of Joyce's genius, found him in certain respects an example of what to avoid. At the University of Virginia in 1957 Faulkner insisted upon the writer's obligation to be comprehensible: "He doesn't have to write it in the way that every idiot can understand it— every imbecile in the third grade can understand it, but he's got to use a language which is accepted and in which the words have specific meanings that everybody agrees on. I think that *Finnegans Wake* and *Ulysses* were justified, but then it's hard to say on what terms they were justified. That was a case of a genius who was electrocuted by the divine fire." [11] With characteristic thrift Faulkner stored away that last phrase and made it part of his stock reply to subsequent questions about Joyce. Fourteen months later he produced the formula without the preparatory justification and felt obliged to add a brief explanation that has an interest of its own: "James Joyce was one of the great men of my time. He was electrocuted by the divine fire. . . . He was probably—might have been the greatest, but he was electrocuted. He had more talent than he could control." [12] This is very close to the criticism Sherwood Anderson had made of Faulkner himself in New Orleans in 1925: "You've got too much talent. You can do it too easy, in too many different ways. If you're not careful, you'll never write anything." [13]

The juxtaposition of the two comments provides an indication of the seductiveness of Joyce's omnipresent example at that moment in the mid-1920s when Faulkner was searching for a specifically contemporary mode—it is tempting to say, a contemporary mould—that would accommodate, shape, and give realization to the rich and various talents he already knew himself to possess. The narrowness of his escape from the dangers of Joycean pastiche can be measured by the obvious derivativeness of sections of *Mosquitoes* and *Flags in the Dust*—the presentation, for instance, of Horace Benbow's reactions as he partners young Frankie at tennis and watches "the taut revelations of her speeding body":

Girlwhite and all thy little   Oh. Not pink no. For a moment
I thought she'd no. Disgraceful, her mamma would call it. Or

any other older woman. Belle's are pink   O muchly
"Oaten reed above the lyre," Horace chanted, catching the
ball at his shoe-tops with a full swing, watching it duck
viciously beyond the net. Oaten reed above the lyre. And
Belle like a harped gesture, not sonorous. Piano, perhaps.
Blended chords, anyway. Unchaste   ? Knowledgeable
better. Knowingly wearied. Wearied knowing. Yes, piano.
Fugue. Fugue of discontent. O moon rotting waxed overlong
too long[14]

It is arguable that such passages are deliberately parodic, inviting
us to watch and mock what might be called the slack revelations
of Horace's ponderous mind. Even so, the excision of this particular passage from the version of *Flags* published as *Sartoris* can be
reckoned one of the more fortunate episodes in the history of that
long-suffering text.

In the years following the spectacular technical experimentation of *The Sound and the Fury* and *As I Lay Dying* Faulkner
seems, on the whole, to have engaged in a deliberate suppression
of identifiably Joycean elements in his language and technique,
and his comments in interviews of the 1950s indicate that while
he acknowledged Joyce as a powerful influence he did not think
of him as one of his masters. Nor, for that matter, did he so regard
Mann or Proust, or any of the lesser "moderns" to whom he was
indebted in minor ways at various points in his career—Aldous
Huxley is an obvious example mentioned by several critics;
Thomas Beer and James Branch Cabell were cited by Faulkner
himself;[15] one might add Elizabeth Madox Roberts, whose *The
Time of Man*[16] probably contributed something to Faulkner's
perception of the southern poor white as a subject for fictional
treatment, and even so unlikely a figure as James Warner Bellah,
convincingly identified by Richard T. Dillon as providing Faulkner with a direct model for at least one of his early short stories.[17]
Such writers, for all their differences one from another, belonged
for Faulkner in the category of "contemporaries," those whom

he had read when his own career was "already fixed," and whose influence therefore did not extend beyond matters of technical detail.

Faulkner's definition of "contemporary" did not, however, embrace Joseph Conrad, whom he seems to have thought of chiefly as the author of *The Nigger of the "Narcissus," Lord Jim,* and *Nostromo,* and hence as having written "towards the top of his talent" in the early years of the twentieth century, when he himself was still a child. He was well aware that Conrad had died in 1924, before the beginning of his own career as a writer of fiction: he had in his library an account of Conrad's funeral, first published in 1925.[18] He may even have visited Conrad's grave in the Roman Catholic cemetery at Canterbury during his brief visit to England in the fall of 1925: "The country is beautiful—south-eastern England: county of Kent," he wrote home from Tunbridge Wells on 9 October 1925, adding: "No wonder Joseph Conrad could write fine books here." [19] It was thus natural enough for Faulkner to view Conrad as a master rather than a contemporary, and such a categorization is already evident in the early linking of the *Nigger* with *Moby-Dick* as books he would have liked to have written and in the naming of Conrad in a draft introduction to *The Sound and the Fury* as one of the authors who provided the scale by which he learned to judge his own work.[20]

Conrad's direct influence is detectable in a number of Faulkner's novels: to the examples mentioned by Adams[21] might be added the correspondences between Quentin Compson and Martin Decoud, the self-doubting intellectual who commits suicide in *Nostromo,* between the fate of Sutpen's design and the corruption of Charles Gould's idealism, and between the Caddy-Benjy relationship in *The Sound and the Fury* and the Winnie-Stevie relationship in *The Secret Agent.* But Conrad's more substantial importance—what gave him magisterial status in Faulkner's imagination—was at the most fundamental levels of structural conception: Albert Guerard, for example, has argued that Conrad's *Chance* constitutes the fullest anticipation of Faulkner's extension of the impressionistic method in *Absalom, Absalom!*[22] David L. Minter speaks of both *Absalom* and *Lord Jim* as novels employing "interpreted design" as a structural principle,[23] and it is certainly possible to see Quentin's obsession with Sutpen as closely akin to Marlowe's fascination with Jim and both works as organized around the centrality of an ultimately "inscrutable" enigma.[24] Yet *Absalom* is an absolutely individual work, and Faulkner moves in these matters with an assured independence that is grounded in an absorption not so much of the specific Conradian method as of the overall Conradian example of bold and deliberate structural command. One might even speculate that the combination of a Conradian structural conception with Joycean narrative techniques which provided the basis for the creative breakthrough that Faulkner achieved in *The Sound and the Fury.*

But Faulkner was conscious from very early on of a still more formidable precedent—more distant in time, but more available in terms of nationality—in the work of Herman Melville, and above all in *Moby-Dick.* Since Faulkner spoke so highly of *Moby-Dick* in early interviews and specifically acknowledged, a quarter of a century later, that much of the moral patterning of *A Fable* had been derived from what he called the "trilogy of conscience" in that same novel,[25] there can be no doubt of Melville's having remained an active presence in his imagination to the very end of his career—which is not necessarily to accept the proposition that he did indeed read *Moby-Dick* "every year." Critics have often seen parallels between the hunt for Old Ben and the hunt for the White Whale, between Cash Bundren and the carpenter on the *Pequod,* between Sutpen and Ahab, between Benjy and Pip, between the General/Corporal relationship in *A Fable* and the Captain Vere/Billy Budd relationship, even between Ratliff the sewing-machine salesman and Melville's lightning-rod man.[26] At a profounder level, perhaps, are the threads that tie some of Faulkner's recurrent character-types to their

Melvillean ancestors—Gavin Stevens and Quentin Compson, for example, to Melville's suspect bachelors, Ike McCaslin and Gail Hightower to the still more radical negativism of Bartleby. But the most striking indication of Melville's importance for Faulkner is supplied by the latter's response, in 1927, to the request of the book editor of the *Chicago Tribune* that he specify the book he would most like to have written:

> I think that the book which I put down with the unqualified
> thought "I wish I had written that" is *Moby Dick*. The Greek-
> like simplicity of it: a man of forceful character driven by
> his sombre nature and his bleak heritage, bent on his own
> destruction and dragging his immediate world down with
> him with a despotic and utter disregard of them as individu-
> als; the fine point to which the various natures caught (and
> passive as though with a foreknowledge of unalterable doom)
> in the fatality of his blind course are swept—a sort of Golgo-
> tha of the heart become immutable as bronze in the sonority
> of its plunging ruin; all against the grave and tragic rhythm
> of the earth in its most timeless phase: the sea.[27]

Not the least remarkable aspect of this altogether remarkable document—the most powerful piece of rhetoric Faulkner had thus far produced—is that the second sentence of the paragraph quoted sounds (until its last word is reached) astonishingly like an evocation of the central narrative movement of *Absalom, Absalom!* Melville's example may have merged with Conrad's insofar as it encouraged Faulkner to make sweeping structural, symbolic, and indeed verbal gestures. But Melville was probably the principal inspiration for what has sometimes been referred to as Faulkner's "Gothicism" and, in general, for his creation of larger-than-life figures, his persistent deployment of extreme forms of language, image, and action, and his radical departures from conventional patterns of logical coherence and stylistic decorum. "I think," said Faulkner at the University of Virginia, "that the moment in the book, the story, demands its own style and seems to me just as natural as the moment in the year produces the leaves. That when Melville becomes Old Testament, Biblical, that seems natural to me. When he becomes Gothic, that seems natural to me, too, and I hadn't, really hadn't stopped to think, Now where does one change and become another?"[28] Melville, in fact, was the master who taught Faulkner most clearly and emphatically that the forms of fiction were not fixed but truly protean, capable of infinite evolution in response to evolving creative needs, and who showed that a writer with sufficient ability and courage could do almost anything with the novel and get away with it—so long as he was prepared to look to the judgment of posterity for confirmation of his success. It is small wonder that Faulkner should have hung one of Rockwell Kent's woodcuts of Ahab on the wall of the living room at Rowanoak.

The particular importance for Faulkner of the other masters whom he was accustomed to acknowledge along with Conrad and Melville—Cervantes, Dickens and Dostoevsky, Balzac and Flaubert—need not be explored in detail here. Although Faulkner evidently admired Cervantes as a great pioneer of the novel form, *Don Quixote* seems to have served him chiefly as the source of the character-type most fully and persistently realized in the figure of Gavin Stevens. His affinities with Dickens and Dostoevsky have been much discussed by critics, and Albert Guerard has discerned in all three novelists a common openness to technical innovation, linguistic extravagance, and extremes of presented experience.[29] Although Faulkner's awareness of French literature deserves far closer study than it has yet received, it seems safe to say that he saw in Flaubert a type of the complete artist, absolutely dedicated to his craft, absolutely in control of every aspect of his work. The passage about Melville's style, already quoted in part, concludes with a contrasting comment on Flaubert: "Though with the *Bovary* it's as though you know from the very first as soon as you see what he's going to do that he will never disappoint you, that it'll be as absolute as mathematics."[30] The broad similarities between Balzac's *La Comédie humaine* and Faulkner's Yoknapatawpha fiction have long been recognized, but he seems also to have valued in Balzac the sheer scope and continuity of an ambition pursued with inexhaustible inventiveness but without stylistic ingratiation—in an interview of 1952 he refers to "Balzac, whose way of writing everything bluntly with the stub of his pen[cil] I admire very much."[31]

Faulkner's appropriation of that last phrase from Somerset Maugham's *Cakes and Ale*[32] may serve as a timely reminder that he was actually and potentially subject to many influences not customarily considered in discussions of his work—although Maugham was in fact mentioned during one of the Nagano seminars and again at Virginia, where he was linked with Henry James as someone who wrote at too great a distance from actual living.[33] Faulkner's attitude to James himself seems somewhat inconsistent—on another Virginia occasion James was praised for the vitality of his characterization, along with other "masters from whom we learned our craft"[34]—and might well repay both a closer and a more extensive scrutiny. Thackeray's name also appears in that same list, but there is otherwise little specific evidence of Faulkner's familiarity with his work and one can only guess at the possible connections between the creation of Benjy Compson and his teasing keeper in *The Sound and the Fury* and the presentation of Sir Pitt Crawley and his bullying nurse in *Vanity Fair*:

> Lady Jane always walked by the old man; and was an evident favourite with him. He used to nod many times to her and smile when she came in, and utter inarticulate deprecatory moans when she was going away. When the door shut upon her he would cry and sob—whereupon Hester's [the nurse's] face and manner, which was always exceedingly bland and gentle while her lady was present, would change at once and she would make faces at him and clench her fist, and scream out, "Hold your tongue, you stoopid old fool," and twirl away

his chair from the fire which he loved to look at—at which he would cry more.[35]

Faulkner may have been too conscious of standing in opposition to the historical traditions associated with Scott to have recognized him as a master, but his almost complete avoidance of Hardy's name—about whom, it is only fair to add, his interviewers never asked him—sorts oddly with the close correspondences between Yoknapatawpha and Wessex as richly imagined and self-consistent fictional worlds. Still incompletely understood, too, is Faulkner's complex relationship—strangely compounded of apprenticeship and rejection, loyalty and rebellion—with Sherwood Anderson. At quite another level of inquiry, it is puzzling to know how much weight, and of what kind, to give to some of the books that apparently date from Faulkner's childhood. How, for example, is it possible to tell or guess the permanent effect upon Faulkner's imagination of a book such as *Classic Tales and Old-Fashioned Stories* (volume 3 of the *Young Folks Treasury*), published in 1909 and edited by Hamilton Wright Mabie and Daniel Edwin Wheeler,[36] which contains, along with much else, simplified extracts not only from *Don Quixote* but also from *Gulliver's Travels, The Arabian Nights, The Iliad, The Odyssey, Robinson Crusoe, The Canterbury Tales,* and *The Pilgrim's Progress*? It is Faulkner himself, once again, who brings out the fascination, the inexhaustibility, and the too frequent inconclusiveness of such inquiries and speculations: "Probably no writer can say, 'I was influenced by so and so.' He can say, of course, 'So and so encouraged me, I admired his work,' and he might say, 'I was influenced by him and no one else.' But that writer is wrong, he is influenced by every word he ever read, I think, every sound he ever heard, every sense he ever experienced; and he is so busy writing that he hasn't time to stop and say, 'Now, where did I steal this from?' But he did steal it somewhere."[37]

What Faulkner's own distinction between masters and contemporaries enables us to perceive, however, is that the blatancy and detectability of any particular theft is likely to bear an inverse relationship to its importance. It is true that Faulkner's astonishingly retentive memory—whose importance he acknowledges—sometimes led him into kleptomaniac borrowings even from the predecessors he most admired. But while he can be caught out in his petty thieveries, precisely because they were so often specific, concrete, and direct, the very profundity and comprehensiveness of his grander larcenies make them far more difficult to pin down. Some of them, indeed, might have remained entirely unknown had they not been made the subject of Faulknerian confessionals characteristically blended not only of honesty and generosity but also of justified arrogance. Masters bestow dignity on their pupils, after all, and it is no small thing to have served an apprenticeship to Melville, Conrad, Balzac, Flaubert, Dickens, Dostoevsky, Cervantes—to name but the named.

Undue Process: Faulkner and
the Law

William Faulkner was no stranger to courtrooms or to
members of the legal profession. Although he never received any formal training in the law—or in anything
much else, for that matter—he seems to have possessed a
considerably better knowledge of it than the average lay-
man, especially of statutes specific to his native state of
Mississippi. He was, as an article by a law professor in
the *Mississippi College Law Review* puts it, "an excellent 'curbstone lawyer,'"[1] what might in other contexts
be called a sea or barrackroom lawyer or, in Faulkner's
own corner of the world, a sawmill advocate. There were
several lawyers in his family—a great-grandfather, a
grandfather, an uncle, and a first cousin—and during his
teens and twenties he spent a good deal of time in the
Oxford, Mississippi, law office of Phil Stone, the closest
of his friends at that period and the strongest of his admirers. It is impossible to determine the sources of any
given aspect of his legal knowledge. We simply do not
know how much reading he did of the law books in
Stone's office, how many legal anecdotes he heard from
Stone or from his own relatives, how many cases he

attended in the Lafayette County courthouse, or how aware of local property law he became during the course of his own land purchases in the Oxford area. But lawyers, legal questions, and actual trial situations certainly appear again and again in his fiction, and the article in the *Mississippi College Law Review* is concerned to demonstrate that his legal references of every sort tend to be more accurate than otherwise.

For lawyers, however, such assurances turn out to be somewhat less than reassuring. In Faulkner's work the persistent failure and even perversion of the legal system serves again and again as both symptom and symbol of a profounder malaise within society at large. The arguments of lawyers and the decisions of judges rarely address the needs, the desires, or even the basic social and economic situations of those seeking justice at their hands. Those with responsibility tend to be corrupted by money or fear or, at the very least, by instinctive identification with the interests of the social or racial group to which they themselves belong or aspire. Legal sophistication is not much in evidence in rural Mississippi—or at any rate in that fictional county Faulkner called Yoknapatawpha—and even when local justices are well-meaning and fundamentally sympathetic to those seeking redress, they are likely to be terrified by the complexity of the issues demanding resolution, dismayed by their own ignorance of the applicable law, and driven to take refuge in narrow and excessively literal interpretations that have the effect of exalting property rights over human rights, or at least over humane considerations. Petitioners, therefore, rarely if ever receive redress. Justice is seen to have been flagrantly not done. Lawyers, attorneys, and judges have for the most part surrendered long ago to a comfortable, self-protective cynicism, only occasional individuals continuing to cherish an idealism that in practice—certainly in their own practices—proves unsustainable, self-defeating, and even actively destructive.

The principal exhibit here must surely be *Sanctuary*, published in 1931, at a moment when Faulkner was at the height of his creative powers. After *The Sound and the Fury*, the first of the indisputably major texts, came the brilliant short novel *As I Lay Dying*, and after *As I Lay Dying* came *Sanctuary*, to be followed in its turn by *Light in August*, another of the acknowledged Faulknerian peaks. The sequence of publication at this point in Faulkner's career is somewhat misleading, however, in that *Sanctuary* was not only finished but submitted to the publisher *ahead* of *As I Lay Dying* and (as I suggested earlier) may have existed in some preliminary form even before the writing of *The Sound and the Fury*. Just why *Sanctuary* was not published when first submitted is by no means clear, although it is possible and indeed tempting to speculate that the publisher may have been somewhat daunted by the violence contained in the book and especially by the directness and specificity with which that violence was presented. What is known is that, when the galley proofs eventually came into Faulkner's hands, he decided that the book was unsatisfactory as it stood and embarked upon a thorough revision of the entire text, one that involved a good deal of rewriting and structural reorganization. The consequent resetting of type also cost him money that he could at that time ill afford, although once *Sanctuary* was finally published he more than recovered his losses in terms both of strong sales and of the Hollywood assignments that came his way as a result of the mildly scandalous publicity the novel attracted.

The novel as Faulkner first wrote it[2] opened with a scene closely corresponding to the beginning of chapter 16 of the published book[3]—with Horace Benbow visiting Goodwin in jail and attempting to reconstruct the events leading up to Tommy's murder. Many of the other crucial narrative events have already occurred by this point in the book's chronology, and the prospective reader of the original version was to have been introduced to them retrospectively, sometimes in quite cumbersome ways. The technique, probably originating in Faulkner's reading of Joseph Conrad, was one that he used with great success on other occasions (in *Light in August*, for example), but in this early instance he did not handle it especially well. Apparently recognizing this when the proofs arrived, he tore the book apart and then put it together again in more or less chronological order, using as his new opening the brilliantly conceived spring-side confrontation between Benbow and Popeye that had formerly been located in the second chapter.

The famous—or perhaps infamous—introduction Faulkner wrote for the Modern Library issue of *Sanctuary* in 1932 gave the impression that the revision process also diminished the violence of a story he claimed to have written out of the crudest of economic motives: "To me it is a cheap idea, because it was deliberately conceived to make money. . . . I took a little time out, and speculated what a person in Mississippi would believe to be current trends, chose what I thought was the right answer and invented the most horrific tale I could imagine." [4] But that introduction was intended to be tongue-in-cheek, though it has rarely been read that way, and comparison of the original and final versions of the novel shows a very different situation. Not only is the original *Sanctuary* a thoroughly serious piece of writing but all the scenes that made the book notorious when it was first published and that led an influential reviewer to categorize Faulkner as a member of the "cruel school" of American literature, a "prime example of American sadism" [5]—all the episodes of the rape and its aftermath, the scene of Red's funeral and all those in the brothel—were in fact carry-overs from that first version, with little or no alteration. Indeed, the violence of the second version was actually increased by the greater directness with which the lynching of Goodwin was presented and by the addition of the bizarre flashback into Popeye's childhood.

Clearly, the violence in the novel was not simply a gimmick for increasing sales but, as Faulkner so often said in later years, a novelistic tool, a means toward a larger end, a fundamental element in his overall conception of the world he wanted to portray. It seems equally clear that, while Faulkner was primarily offering in the novel a radical criticism of his own Mississippi society and what Horace Benbow at one point sourly refers to as its "free Democratico-Protestant atmosphere," [6] he was at the same time using the linked, abstractable themes of violence and injustice as a means of pointing to a kind of corruption and cynicism that he saw as pervasive of American society as a whole. The novel is, after all, absolutely contemporary in its setting, and it speaks, as such, to a moment in American history characterized by economic depression, by prohibition laws whose unpopularity and unenforceability brought the entire legal system into contempt, and by the spectacular gangsterism prohibition did so much to promote and sustain. It seems entirely relevant that Memphis should be a big city beyond (if only just beyond) the actual boundaries of Mississippi, as well as beyond the notional boundaries of Yoknapatawpha County, and that Popeye should have been based quite closely on a well-known Memphis underworld figure, Neil Karens "Popeye" Pumphrey, who evaded conviction for the various murders of which he was from time to time accused and then died, apparently by his own hand, in October 1931, just a few months before *Sanctuary* first appeared. Faulkner reportedly got the story of rape and abduction from a woman encountered in a Memphis bar who had been Pumphrey's victim in real life,[7] and it could conceivably have been the fear of a response from Pumphrey, in the form of a libel action, or worse, that caused the book's publication to be held up.

Although the action of the novel is thus in many respects time-specific, it undoubtedly raises, often in profoundly ironic terms, a number of persistently relevant questions about the judicial process, about crime and punishment, and about responsibility and guilt. What are readers to think and feel, for example, about Popeye's dodging so many penalties that might be thought of as "just" only to suffer at the end of the novel a form of judicial murder for a crime he did not in fact commit? And how are responses to the manner of his death modified or complicated by the suspicion that it represents for Popeye himself a form of tidy suicide? "Fix my hair, Jack," he says as the trap is sprung[8]—an episode, incidentally, that appears in the original text and could not, therefore, have been added after the "real-life" Pumphrey suicide. To what extent, again, is the sense of Popeye's responsibility for his crimes, including his crimes against Temple, affected by the revelation of his childhood history that Faulkner added to the final chapter of the published version? Given the predominantly comic manner of its telling, can that flashback even be taken seriously as a case history?

Where, in particular, does the primary responsibility lie for what happens to Temple? Is Popeye really the villain? How much responsibility should Gowan Stevens bear for so messily bringing the whole situation into being in the first place? Or does much of the blame lie with Temple herself, arrogant as she is in her sense of middle-class superiority and security ("My father's a judge")[9] and provocative in her empty automatic coquettishness? How, indeed, should Temple be regarded throughout the whole sequence of her experiences? Is she to be condemned, as she was by many early critics, for displaying a total lack of discretion and an actual affinity for evil, or should she rather be seen as so crippled by her patriarchal background and so traumatized by the rape and by everything that follows that she is effectively deprived of all responsibility for her actions? Does Faulkner's presentation of her not confront the reader, in fact, with many of the dilemmas more recently associated with such a figure as Patty Hearst?

There are also a number of more specifically legal or lawyerly issues that seem to arise from the book. At one level, of course, it can simply be said that the entire system of justice, of law and order, is inextricably implicated in the social and moral corruption that comprehensively riddles the novel's presented world. Judges use their power and influence to circumvent due process. District attorneys seek convictions on any terms and for purely personal ends. Lawyers, purchasable either by money or by sex, operate by secret manipulation rather than by courtroom argument and are often as corrupt as the clients they serve. (Horace's assertion that there is an inevitable corruption involved in trafficking with evil would seem, if valid, to cast a doubtful shadow over criminal lawyers in general). Along with police chiefs and detectives, lawyers seem also to provide Miss Reba's brothel with some of its best and most regular customers—among them "the biggest lawyer in Memphis" who earns his superlative not only by being a millionaire but by weighing "two hundred and eighty pounds" and having his own special bed installed.[10] Horace's assurance to Goodwin that he can count on the protection of "law, justice, civilization"[11] turns out in practice to be disastrously and culpably naive, as does almost everything else said and done by the novel's one example of a well-meaning man of law.

Horace's pampered and self-pitying ineffectuality—so sharply set off against Ruby's resourceful coping with hardship—is brought out in the early scenes of his talking and drinking too much while at the Old Frenchman place. Ruby's assessment of him at that time is much shrewder than his assessment of her, whom he tends to see as a damsel in distress, a cause to fight for, an occasion to set out on a knightly quest for justice and truth. But strong as he may be on the ethics of his profession, Horace is altogether shakier when it comes to matters of actual practice. Indeed, practicing law is what he appears to have done very little of: nothing seems to prevent his simply walking away from either home or office in Kinston, and although Miss Jenny says that even Horace must have some business back there, it is not at all clear that he does. It is also Miss Jenny who has to remind him of the need to observe basic professional proprieties in his relations with Ruby. As the novel proceeds Horace has occasion to measure the gulf that divides his limp idealism from the harsh realities of a society whose moral elevation can be measured in terms of its election and toleration of a state senator such as Clarence Snopes. At Goodwin's trial he finds himself standing helplessly and almost wordlessly by while events are grossly manipulated by Eustace Graham and then grotesquely sanctioned by that dignified representative of the legal profession Judge Drake—supported, of course, by his phalanx of sons, at least two of whom are lawyers themselves.[12] (The son still at Yale may yet become a lawyer, presumably, especially since Faulkner's early supporter Phil Stone went there for one of his law degrees.)

While much in the trial scene remains obscure, to the point that it becomes difficult to determine what, if any, prescribed procedures are in fact being followed, it is at least crystal clear that Horace proves himself hopelessly incompetent as a defense lawyer. It has to be said for Horace that he has arrayed against him a series of forces at once more numerous and more formidable than he could ever have hoped to contend with: Popeye, of course, who has shot Red just a few days earlier, of whom Temple is presumably afraid, and for whom the Memphis lawyer is evidently working; Eustace Graham, seeking a conviction at any cost, secretly abetted by Horace's own sister and perhaps by the Memphis lawyer; and Temple's family, headed by Judge Drake, superficially the very type of southern judgeship and gentlemanliness but in practice concerned only to defend his family's name. It is Horace, however, who refuses to allow Goodwin to make the guilty plea that the latter believes (rightly, as it turns out) could save his life, who allows Ruby on the first day of the trial to mention Temple as part of her evidence, and who calls Temple as a witness for the defense—only to be stunned into impotent silence when she perjures herself in such absolute terms.

It appears from the reference to her "parrotlike answers" and to Graham's concern with "holding her eyes"[13] that Temple has been "got at" by the prosecution and drilled to give a series of prepared answers designed to get an easy conviction—and simultaneously protect Popeye—by throwing on Goodwin the blame not only for Tommy's murder but for the rape as well; those same answers also serve to minimize her own, hence her family's public shame by avoiding all reference to Miss Reba's and the life she had led there. Some commentators think that when Temple is asked where she has been living she supplies Miss Reba's address, but it seems more likely, especially in light of her earlier reference to Memphis as her present "home" and of Graham's use of the term "in hiding,"[14] that she would have given instead either a fictitious address or the actual address to which she was taken following Popeye's shooting of Red on 17 June—evidently the event to which Miss Reba refers when Horace telephones to check on Temple's whereabouts immediately before the opening of the trial (on 20 June) and she asks him, "Dont you read no papers?"[15]

Horace's collapse at the moment of crisis is generally read as a failure of character, an almost inevitable consequence of his fundamental ineffectuality and of a set of professional and class assumptions and attitudes toward women that prevent him from ever imagining that other representatives of law and justice could behave in so corrupt and ungentlemanly a fashion or that so signal a representative of an apotheosized Southern Womanhood as Temple Drake could prove so dishonest in the witness-box. Joseph R. Urgo, however, has argued[16] that the question of Temple's perjury is less straightforward than normally assumed, and although he fails to acknowledge the occasions when she does lie outright—for example, in her direct, deliberate, and unqualified statement that Goodwin shot Tommy—Urgo is certainly correct in insisting that when Temple says at the trial that it was Goodwin from whom she was hiding in the crib, she is stating no more than the truth.[17] Goodwin, as Ruby immediately recognized, was as aware of Temple's attraction as any of the other men at the Old Frenchman place, and although it is unclear whether Tommy is speaking on his own or on Goodwin's behalf (or on behalf of them both) when he offers Temple the dubious reassurance that "Lee says hit wont hurt you none. All you got to do is lay down,"[18] the very quotation of these words as originating with Goodwin lends support to Urgo's basic argument that Temple was already thoroughly terrorized before the actual rape occurred, that Goodwin had participated in that terrorization (even though, as the dominant presence at the Old Frenchman place, he could have protected Temple had he chosen to do so), that the guilt for Temple's violation was thus by no means confined to Popeye himself, and that Goodwin specifically, while technically innocent of the rape, certainly bore a portion of the responsibility for the overall sequence of events. Urgo also hints, though he does not quite say, that there may have been an element of revenge in Temple's courtroom performance—that, given an opportunity to exact retribution from at least one of her terrorizers, she does not hesitate to seize it.

In a sense, of course, these arguments are rather beside the legal, or at any rate the courtroom, point. Goodwin is formally on trial for the murder of Tommy, and on that issue Temple clearly does perjure herself—always assuming, of course, that she retains any clear memory of the whole disastrous train of events: the final scene in the Luxembourg Gardens, often read as emblematic of Temple's immunity from the consequences of the novel's action, can no less plausibly be viewed as indicative of long-term traumatization. The whole character and direction of Goodwin's trial—even, it could be said, its entire claim to be considered a legal proceeding—is distorted and subverted in a moment by the introduction of the rape element, and especially of the blood-stained corncob said to have been used in the assault. It is even necessary to have some sympathy for Horace's predicament if one assumes that he was indeed taken entirely by surprise by a deliberate and cynical prosecution tactic, presumably prompted by Narcissa's tip-off to Eustace Graham and obviously calculated to arouse the jury's emotions to the point of obscuring the lack of evidence relevant to the murder itself. Whether Horace *ought* to have been taken by surprise after his own interview with Temple is quite another matter—it can be argued[19] that he was in any case disabled by rape fantasies of his own in which the image of Temple merged with that of his obsessively desired stepdaughter Little Belle. The fact apparently remains (there is again no direct textual evidence) that he immediately realizes that the corncob tactic will work—that in a society dedicated to the sanctification of Southern Womanhood it cannot fail to work—and therefore, without speaking another word, lets what he recognizes as an inevitable process take its headlong and ultimately violent course.

Faulkner perhaps counted upon his readers also recognizing what would happen once the corncob had been introduced into evidence, and he would not have wanted to blur the issue by narrating stages in the trial that lacked emotional or even thematic significance. What he needed to dramatize—without too much disturbing the crisp narrative pace maintained in the book as a whole—was simply the corrupt alliance of the properly constituted legal guardians of Yoknapatawpha County against Horace's well-meaning but culpable and, for Goodwin, fatal incompetence. The handling of the trial does, even so, seem remarkably scanty and inexpressive, although the fact that the original text of the novel is no clearer at these points seems to leave open the possibility that Faulkner thought he was offering a not excessively caricatured representation of how such a trial might indeed have proceeded in a Mississippi courtroom of that date—a date, certainly, at which lynchings (if almost always of blacks) were by no means unknown in the Deep South.

Sanctuary is perhaps a special case among Faulkner's novels, insofar as it seems to have been written almost as a deliberate exercise, at once horrific and subversively comic, in the grotesquerie of violence and judicial corruption. But there is no shortage of other novels and stories by Faulkner in which lawyers, judges, or justices of the peace play significant roles. Although Horace Benbow did not reappear in later novels, he was replaced in Faulkner's battery of recurring characters by another lawyer, Gavin Stevens, who combined much of Horace's romantic idealism with considerably greater legal and especially courtroom competence. Stevens appears in several of Faulkner's books. *Light in August*, the earliest of these, is profoundly concerned with crime and punishment, but not especially with legal process, and Stevens remains a minor character. He similarly appears in only the final section of *Go Down, Moses*, although that novel again touches upon many issues—most of them relating to the practical and moral implications of inheritance—that the law attempts to address. In the more polemical *Intruder in the Dust*, however, Stevens is centrally important as the lawyer who proceeds on the assumption of his black client's guilt until a small boy proves him wrong.

In *Knight's Gambit* Stevens plays, more or less honorably, the central investigatory role in a series of detective stories, characteristically proving his point in highly manipulated courtroom situations. And in the second and third novels of the "Snopes" trilogy, which engages throughout with practical and sometimes technical questions of local property law, Stevens appears in modified Benbovian guise as an idealist who repeatedly renders himself ineffective—both as man and as lawyer—by his failure to take sufficiently into account either the complexities of human nature or the practical realities of the society in which he lives. In the final novel, *The Mansion*, his idealism itself is called into question by his participation in securing, on compassionate grounds, the release from prison of an elderly murderer (Mink Snopes) who will inevitably seek to kill the man he believes responsible for his forty years' incarceration—the very man whom Stevens himself has for an even longer period regarded with profound personal contempt and extravagant social terror.

Most interesting in relation to *Sanctuary* is *Requiem for a Nun*, in which, as we have seen, some of the events and moral issues of *Sanctuary* are revisited from the narrative perspective of some eight years later. The core of *Requiem* consists of a series of scenes in which Stevens, although not in an actual courtroom, persistently and often brutally cross-examines Temple (now married to Gowan Stevens) as to her experiences in Miss Reba's brothel and her degree of responsibility for the violent events that occurred at that time and, more especially, since. Although it may sound from this account that Stevens in effect avails himself of the opportunity that his predecessor, Horace Benbow, so signally failed to grasp, there are too many differences between the two novels—written some twenty years apart—for the one to be read at all straightforwardly as a commentary on the other. What does, however, seem of some significance for a reading of *Sanctuary* is the fact that the Stevens of *Requiem for a Nun* is by no means a wholly positive figure. Interpretations of the novel have varied widely, and many commentators, indeed, have shrewdly dodged confronting it at all. But recent criticism of *Requiem*, following Noel Polk, has tended to the view that it is Temple who emerges the more sympathetically precisely because she does not, like Stevens, brood obsessively on the past but makes a genuine attempt—late and desperate though it may be, and possibly doomed—to escape from that burden and make for herself and those close to her the best life she can. Stevens's insistence in *Requiem* on the letter of the moral law is reminiscent of the self-defeating rigidity of Benbow's specifically legal assumptions in *Sanctuary* itself, and both attitudes seem consistent with Faulkner's persistent representation of lawyers and the law as insufficiently related to life either as it is or as it should be. (It is amusing, and characteristically Faulknerian, that in a novel that might almost serve as a temperance tract Popeye is the only nondrinker: "There ought to be a law," he declares,[20] meaning a law against drinking and quite charmingly overlooking not only the fact that such a law notoriously does exist but that he himself, as a bootlegger, is dedicated to its universal evasion. Horace, too, in what functions as a deliberate echo, thinks there should be a law against the disturbing sexuality of summer nights.)[21]

Faulkner, an essentially conservative thinker, certainly saw the law as crucial to the maintenance of social order and was in no sense concerned to challenge or subvert either its functions or its enshrined values. He probably did not even entertain any special hostility toward judges and lawyers as a group: nobody else in his novels and stories does much better—apart, perhaps, from the truly innocent, a category from which many more than lawyers must be considered automatically disbarred. But to be thus committed to the law was to become the more sensitive to its abuse, and Faulkner seized almost inevitably upon the unique reticulations of the legal system—its constant institutionalized interactions between the powerful and the powerless, the socially gracious and the socially disgraced—as providing narrative materials and sources of symbolic reference precisely suited to writing about the sickness of specific societies or about the universal experience of human mischancing, the failure of things to be or to turn out as they should. If, in *Sanctuary* and elsewhere, Faulkner's world seems structured upon the relationship—at once intimate and distant—between the panoply of the courthouse and the squalor of the jail, that is perhaps only another element in his fundamental recognition of the necessary coexistence and countervailing polarity of human (and especially societal) aspiration and human (and especially individual) defeat.

Unreal Estate: Reflections on Wessex and Yoknapatawpha

Most people, confronted by the juxtaposition of the names of Thomas Hardy and William Faulkner, are likely to be struck by the obvious contrasts between them—the differences of nationality, region, period, technique, and so on. But before turning to the reasons why I believe it may be instructive to consider them together, it is perhaps worth pausing for a moment to review some of the curious points of similarity in their lives and careers. Although Faulkner was so much the younger of the two—having been born in 1897, the year in which Hardy published the book version of his last novel, *The Well-Beloved*—they were for a brief moment literary contemporaries, Faulkner's first novel appearing in 1926, two years before Hardy's death. They were both small men, well below the average in height; both largely self-educated; both unhappy in marriage; both intensely private, always fighting off the intrusions of interviewers and tourists and would-be biographers. It was Hardy who achieved the ultimate in evasive tactics by ghostwriting his own posthumous official biography, but Faulkner gained at least temporary respite by the simple device of permitting the circulation of the wildest kinds of misinformation about himself and his work.

These are not, however, the topics I intend to pursue. Nor is it my purpose to attempt to establish specific links between the two authors—to argue, that is, that Faulkner's work was significantly affected by an awareness of Hardy's. That might at some point be an appropriate subject for speculation, but there is precious little direct evidence to go on. Faulkner did have in his library a copy of the 1917 Modern Library edition of *The Mayor of Casterbridge*, complete with a truly terrible introduction by Joyce Kilmer—who might have done better, perhaps, had he been asked to introduce *The Woodlanders*. And since Faulkner wrote his name in the book in two separate places there is a strong presumption that he read it, probably quite early in his career. He also owned and signed a copy of *Jude the Obscure*.[1] Of more pertinent interest are the broad correspondences between Hardy's fictional Wessex and Faulkner's Yoknapatawpha County and the more specific similarities between the town and community of Casterbridge as presented in *Mayor* and the town and community of Jefferson, especially as presented in *Light in August*. Each novel is central to its region and each, interestingly enough, involves the death of what might in critical shorthand be called a "scapegoat" figure who arrives from elsewhere and eventually suffers communal rejection—although it is surely inevitable that any novelist given to the creation of closed communities, whether regional or otherwise, is likely to deal largely in intruders and intruder plots. There is also the irrefutable though not readily manageable fact that 2 June 1910, the date of the second section of *The Sound and the Fury*, hence of Quentin Compson's death, was also the date of Hardy's seventieth birthday. Was Faulkner engaged in the operation of killing off a literary father? I don't think so, though I suppose it might strengthen or at any rate enliven my case if I did.

To come then, to that case—which will, in truth, be not so much a pleading of a cause as a series of reflections, as advertised in my subtitle, upon the similarities and differences between Hardy and Faulkner as practitioners of regionalism and creators of fictional worlds.

It is, of course, a distressing characteristic, perhaps a basic problem, of regionalism that those who live what are customarily thought of as the most truly regional lives—living and working close to the land, rooted for generations in one dear or dreadful but at any rate perpetual spot—are unlikely to be those who will write about it. They may, however, talk about it, and it is clear that for both Hardy and Faulkner the tradition of local story-telling and the experience of hearing such stories in childhood and early youth was fundamental to the formation of a sense of regional identity. As Ezra Pound so succinctly put it, "The life of a village is narrative"—by which, of course, he meant comprised of well-worn stories about the past and new-minted gossip about the present: "[Y]ou have not been there three weeks before you know that in the revolution et cetera, and when M le Comte et cetera, and so forth." [2] One thinks in this context of the densely evocative passage in *The Woodlanders* that enumerates the elements of "old association" essential to anyone who hopes to escape boredom in a rural spot as lonely as Little Hintock. They must include, the narrator declares,

> an almost exhaustive biographical or historical acquaintance with every object, animate and inanimate, within the observer's horizon. He must know all about those invisible ones of the days gone by, whose feet have traversed the fields which look so grey from his windows; recall whose creaking plough has turned those sods from time to time; whose hands planted the trees that form a crest to the opposite hill; whose horses and hounds have torn through that underwood; what birds affect that particular brake; what bygone domestic dramas of love, jealousy, revenge, or disappointment have been enacted in the cottages, the mansion, the street or on the green. [3]

Landscape itself, this seems to suggest, is significant and apprehensible only to those capable of approaching it as a document in which the skilled reader may discern, faded perhaps but legible still, the records of the local past.

The men and women thus visibly or associatively memorialized are by definition obscure, isolated from the acknowledged main currents and power structures of their time, insignificant in the eyes of the great world, and it is, of course, a part of Hardy's distinction as a novelist that he gives substance and meaning to such lives through the recognition and re-creation of their inherent dramatic patterns. As one who was later to demonstrate that no subject is too trivial for a poem, Hardy had no difficulty in accepting, even embracing, the Wordsworthian proposition that the human passions are no less human or less passionate when experienced by the humble and inarticulate—that they may then appear, indeed, in their sharpest outline. He does not, it is true, treat at length of what he clearly saw as the total economic entrapment and hopeless drudgery of the agricultural labourer, but he returns again and again to the situation of those, male and female, who are of the class of minimally independent tradesmen to which his own father belonged and into which he himself was born—the class of such as Giles Winterborne, Gabriel Oak, and the Dewy family in *Under the Greenwood Tree*, possessed of the potential for at least minor class transitions in either an upward or a downward direction.

Such shifts, so trivial to an external view (including that of Hardy's likely readers in his own time), obviously demanded sustained and detailed treatment in order to establish their importance, their treatability, their potential inclusion among those "dramas of a grandeur and unity truly Sophoclean"[4] that Hardy claimed could occur in the recesses of Wessex. His general procedure as a novelist was therefore one of incremental enlargement, the deployment of the full dramatic and even melodramatic resources of postromantic fiction in the interests of bringing such sequestered spots and unconsidered events sharply and unignorably before the reader's attention. The central Wessex texts are characteristically centered upon small and isolated communities and upon the intensity of social and personal interaction within those communities. Individually the novels tend to be geographically restricted, narrowly focused, and worked out in terms of some combination of a wheel-of-fortune pattern and an intruder plot. Remember, the director Ann Jellicoe is said to have told the author of the Dorchester (alias Casterbridge) community play, community plays are consensus plays, so the villains should always be from out of town.[5] Hardy's novels typically conform to such a model, although on occasion some at least of the disruptive forces may already be physically present within the community but separated from it and from its values by differences in wealth, morality, education, or social class—often by a combination of these.

Hardy, of course, spent his childhood and youth within just such a community. Indeed, he acquired as a child an almost impeccable set of regional credentials—growing up as he did in a splendidly vernacular and romantically, not to say inconveniently, isolated thatched cottage as the child of singing, dancing, storytelling, and musical parents—make that folksinging, folkdancing, folkstorytelling, and folkmusical parents—who, while not themselves of the laboring class, were in social and economic terms only marginally superior to it. That they felt themselves hugely superior I don't doubt—that was what encouraged and enabled Hardy's mother to propel him in the direction of the architectural profession and the middle-class—but the modest heyday of Thomas Hardy senior's prosperity as a builder came at a later date and not during the years of Hardy's own childhood. Hardy soon lost his regional innocence, however. And what corrupted him was not that reputed snobbery upon which, as upon his father's status as a small employer, his recent critics have all too eagerly seized,[6] but, first, the closeness of Bockhampton to a Dorchester that by the late 1840s had advanced, as he himself put it, "to railways and telegraphs and daily London papers,"[7] and, later, his own embarkation upon a process of educational, professional, and social advancement that in his early twenties took him out of Dorset altogether and into London itself.

And yet it was, in a real sense, London that made him a regionalist, as perhaps all regional artists must leave their regions—or come to them from elsewhere—before becoming conscious of their calling. Even William Barnes had been out of Dorset before he became its poet, and the choric figures in *The Mayor of Casterbridge* offer some particularly disenchanted remarks on Farfrae's hard-headed abandonment of the Scotland of which he sings with such soft-hearted longing. It was, at all events, London that first turned Hardy toward the novel, by exposing him to the urban market for fiction and to the possibility of pursuing his own literary ambitions in that direction. It was London, too, that provided him with the perspective from which he would in due course recognize the advantages not only of an essentially rural subject-matter but also of a specific fictional area, geographically defined and distinctively named, that could be explored and exploited in a series of stories over a period of time. That recognition came slowly, even so, and what we know of Hardy's vanished first novel, *The Poor Man and the Lady*, should remind us that there was nothing inevitable about his eventual preoccupation with rural characters in regional settings.

"The series of novels I projected being mainly of the kind called local, they seemed to require a territorial definition of some sort to lend unity to their scene"[8]: so Hardy recalled in the preface to the 1895 edition of *Far from the Madding Crowd*, though with what degree of accuracy it is difficult to estimate. What does seem worth noticing is the element of arbitrariness involved. Whether or not Hardy did, in fact, envisage a whole series of specific novels as early as 1874, it does not sound from this account as though he had at that time any clear conception of the elaborated structure that Wessex would eventually become. He speaks of "local" novels—presumably novels set, like *The Return of the Native, Under the Greenwood Tree, The Woodlanders,*

and *Far from the Madding Crowd* itself, within sharply individu-
alized and narrowly restricted areas—and concerns himself only
secondarily, as a kind of afterthought, with the possibility of
lending unity to their settings by the superimposition of some
sort of "territorial definition." Wessex, that is to say, was not in
itself the initial point of imaginative growth but came into being
as a kind of geographical umbrella organization to which the
separate novels could be as tightly or loosely related as circumstances seemed to dictate. The examples of Scott, Blackmore, and
Trollope must have been in Hardy's mind at this point, together
with the realization—at any rate, the assumption—that people
liked to read about unfamiliar places and little-known social
groups: as he put it in his essay on "The Profitable Reading of
Fiction," "The town man finds what he seeks in novels of the
country." [9] What evidently seemed crucial, even as early as 1874,
was the assertion of an overall name—like the Waverley Novels,
or the Barsetshire Novels, or *La Comédie humaine*—that would
be distinctive in itself and provide an invitation, perhaps even an
incentive, to the reader to move on from one text to another.

That this was a deliberate strategy on Hardy's part is confirmed by his persisting in the invocation of Wessex names and
settings even during those years between *Far from the Madding
Crowd* and *The Mayor of Casterbridge* when he seemed for extended periods to have abandoned altogether any perspective
compatible with the regional stance as customarily understood.
It was, nevertheless, a strategy of which he to some extent lost
control as a consequence of the enthusiasm with which it was
seized upon by his readers, and it can fairly be said that the concept of Wessex at which he had arrived by the later stages of his
career was not only very different from the one he had held in
1874 but was almost as much a creation of his audience and of
the contemporary media as it was of the author himself.

My colleague W. J. Keith wrote several years ago about Hardy's
responsiveness to the "literary pilgrims" who descended upon
Dorchester and its surroundings from the later years of the nine-

teenth century onward,[10] and it is obvious from Hardy's own retrospective comments that he and his work were deeply affected by the extraordinarily rapid acceptance of Wessex as a name for the south-western English portion of the world commonly called real. It was in that 1895 preface to *Far from the Madding Crowd* in particular that he spoke of the way in which the name Wessex, which he had "thought to reserve to the horizons and landscapes of a merely realistic dream-country," had in fact "become more and more popular as a practical provincial definition," with the consequence that "the dream-country has, by degrees, solidified into a utilitarian region which people can go to, take a house in, and write to the papers from. But I ask all good and gentle readers to be so kind as to forget this, and to refuse steadfastly to believe that there are any inhabitants of a Victorian Wessex outside the pages of this and the companion volumes in which they were first discovered."[11] Though humorously phrased, this appeal does show that in 1895, at least, Hardy was perfectly clear as to the necessity of maintaining a sharp distinction between his own created world and those actual locations into which his admirers persisted in pursuing the figments of his imagination.

But the external pressures were very much in the opposite direction. Books and articles about Wessex appeared in profusion, most of them proffering paintings, sketches, or photographs illustrative of "scenes from the Wessex novels," and confident identifications of the "real places" underlying Hardy's often complex fictions. Photographers and interviewers and newspaper paragraphists, as their subject scathingly called them, hunted eagerly for usable material, often infuriating Hardy by their biographical impertinences and their disturbance of his own peace at Max Gate and that of his family still living in the Bockhampton cottage. The pilgrims manifested themselves in the streets of a Dorchester they confusingly insisted on referring to as Casterbridge, and it was not long before the indigenous inhabitants began to reconceive of themselves, individually and even corporately, under such now familiar names as Wessex Motors, the Wessex

Water Board, the Wessex Saddleback Pig Society, the Caster-bridge Hotel, and so on. I've yet to encounter a Jude the Obscure Pork Butchers or a Withered Arm Pharmacy, but they too may be out there somewhere.

The late nineteenth century was a period when regionalism as a cultural, economic, and political concept was very much in the contemporary air, and in asserting such a concept within and through his fiction Hardy was closely aligned with the broader movements of history. Given such pressures from his audience, from the press and from the times themselves—given, too, his own shrewd sense of what was most likely to enhance the con-tinuing sales of his books—it is not surprising that Hardy, who had originally paid little systematic attention to the topographi-cal details of his fictional places, should have begun increasingly to accept, or at any rate entertain, propositions advanced as to the correspondences between scenes in his fiction and towns, villages, buildings, and natural features discoverable on maps and visitable in person. And there seems every reason to sus-pect that he came in the end to develop a genial Scott-like anti-quarian interest in his own accomplished work, considered both as a series of interrelated narratives and as a quasi-historical, quasi-topographical reflection of the world into which he had been born.

It was in the course of the extensive revisions that Hardy made to the Osgood, McIlvaine collected edition of 1895−97 and the Macmillan Wessex Edition of 1912−13 that Wessex eventually evolved into a systematic conceptual unit: not only did all the texts appear in the same published format but they were made more consistent one with another in such matters as the naming of places and the specification of distances. A Wessex map, based on one drawn by Hardy himself, appeared at the back of each volume, and in 1913 Hardy even went so far as to collaborate with his photographer friend Hermann Lea in the production of *Thomas Hardy's Wessex*, a book entirely dedicated to identifying the "originals" of scenes invoked in the stories. As such, it stood as the "official" answer to all such queries and so contributed to the deflection of impertinent inquiries into his own life and up-bringing and especially into that childhood world so defensively cherished in his memory as the source not only of his deepest personal relationships—those with his father, his mother, and his sister Mary—but also of so much of the material from which his novels had been constructed.

Hardy's fiction—including his shorter fiction—is full of ref-erences to local customs, history, traditions, and folklore, and it is characteristic that when questioned as to their source he would often cite the authority of old people he had known. In several instances it is obvious that the information had in fact come from his own father or mother, and I have argued in *Thomas Hardy: A Biography* the proposition that his parents, both in themselves and as the embodiment of memories going back to a time before his own birth, always constituted for him one of the most power-ful—perhaps *the* most powerful—of his imaginative resources. Wessex had always been for Hardy a device for transposing se-lected elements of the real into a mode of existence formally de-clared unreal—fictional, imaginative, a country of dreams. But in its later phases Wessex became increasingly a technique for keeping reality at bay—a means of arresting time, of preserving the treasured past of his parents and of his own childhood and projecting it forward into a future beyond the moment of his own death. Because it thus constituted a kind of temporal suspension, with only a minimum of chronological specificity or perspective, it was inevitably and, I suspect, deliberately elusive of historical definition. Though it might indeed chart a historical process, that is to say, it did not claim or even seek to correlate that process at all precisely with the chronologies of public, of actual history.

It was also vague in terms of spatial integrity. "[T]hings were like that in Wessex," Hardy once declared,[12] but Wessex, as defined by him and represented in the maps he drew, was per-haps too extensive and various to be conceptually grasped by anyone other than a geographer—especially in a country such as

Britain in which differences of just a few miles could (and sometimes still can) make an enormous difference to customs, speech, and local loyalties. But the fact that the Wessex fiction remained as a body somewhat ill-defined did not run counter to Hardy's larger purposes as a regionalist, insofar as it allowed him to comprehend a wide range of essentially local novels within the boundaries of a nominal Wessex and thus project a generalized sense of a rural area with the geographical expansiveness, human density, temporal depth, and socioeconomic distinctiveness sufficient to enable it to be set over against the dominant urban culture of the day—of his day and, even more overwhelmingly, of our own.

William Faulkner stands in a sense between Hardy's day and ours, and many things that in Hardy the late Victorian remain tentative and uncertain are in Faulkner the modernist deliberate and unmistakable. Where Hardy, for instance, found his way very gradually to the evolution of a fictional world that remained, even in its evolved condition, quite loosely organized and only partially integrated, Faulkner seems to have recognized immediately upon becoming a novelist the advantages not only of anchoring his stories in a particular region but also of linking them one to another by specific repetitions and continuities of location, character, and event. That first novel, *Soldiers' Pay*, was set almost exclusively in a small southern town supposed to be situated in the state of Georgia, while his second, *Mosquitoes*, was in a sense even more intensively local, in that the characters he placed on board his contemporary ship of fools constituted a microcosm of the New Orleans literary world he was seeking to satirize. By the time he began his third novel—published in his lifetime only in the shortened version entitled *Sartoris*—Faulkner was already seized with the ambition, and with the strategic conception, of devoting himself to the composition of an entire sequence of novels and stories that would severally and jointly explore the history, topography, and social texture—exploit the narrative possibilities, in short—of the area of northern Mississippi in which he had himself been born and raised.

This may have been a coolly practical decision, based on the examples of such novelists as Scott, Balzac, and James Fenimore Cooper, with all of whom he seems to have been thoroughly familiar. It may even have been inspired in part by knowledge of Hardy's work. It remains in any case true that whereas Hardy had almost to be shown by others what he had in fact achieved in and through his creation of Wessex, Faulkner's creation of Yoknapatawpha County was a matter from the first of profound literary as well as emotional investment. It is not quite certain when he actually named Yoknapatawpha County, but there is no doubt that by the end of the 1920s he had deliberately embarked upon the creation and elaboration of a regionally defined, narratively incremental, and fundamentally symbolic fictional world—upon the realization of his perception that "the whole output or sum of an artist's work had to have a design."[13]

The word "artist" is important there. Whatever extraordinary blend of anxious modesty and sublime vanity Hardy may be imagined as arriving at in old age, when he was beyond question the most famous writer not only in Britain but throughout the world, his literary ambitions in his earlier years seem not to have gone much further than becoming a parson in a retired rural spot and writing in his spare time (obviously projected as considerable) some verses that might or might not be published. Years later he confessed that his greatest hope had been to write one poem good enough to be included in an anthology such as *The Golden Treasury*. Faulkner, on the other hand, was determined to become an artist even before he had any firm ideas as to what kind of art he might best be cut out for, and nobody who knows anything of his biography can doubt for a moment that he formed very early on a high conception both of the artist's role and of his personal capacity to fulfil it. "An artist is a creature driven by demons," Faulkner once said. "He don't know why they choose him and he's usually too busy to wonder why. He is completely amoral in that he will rob, borrow, beg, or steal from anybody and everybody to get the work done." And he added: "If a writer has to rob his mother, he will not hesitate; the *Ode on a*

Grecian Urn is worth any number of old ladies." [14] Nor was this a merely rhetorical statement. I don't mean that he robbed his mother—much of his energy, indeed, was taken up with providing economic support for a whole series of relatives, connections, and family retainers ("parasites," as he said, who did not "even have the grace to be sycophants").[15] But the most unforgettable moment in a television film made about Faulkner a few years ago was his daughter's recollection of his responding to some inconvenient request of hers with the words, "No one remembers Shakespeare's children."

If I emphasize this point, it is not because I do not realize that Hardy, closeted in his study all those years of days, was as ruthless in his way as Faulkner in his. (I can imagine the two Mrs. Hardys nodding their heads in melancholy agreement.) Faulkner's tough-mindedness is important simply because his earlier and greater self-assurance, his sheer determination to match himself against the world's best from Shakespeare on down, had major consequences for his subsequent career and for the character of his created world. Faulkner started out as a poet (as Hardy had done), and throughout his career he continued to speak of himself as a failed poet. The description seems accurate enough, and yet the surviving verse—gauche, derivative, and oddly incoherent as it mostly is—remains interesting for its demonstration of the self-consciously literary attitudes that Faulkner from the very beginning took toward his work, toward the subject-matter of that work, and even toward himself. The sequence of rhyming octosyllabic pastorals that went into that very first volume, *The Marble Faun,* is set in a Pan- and nymph-haunted, relentlessly "sylvan" landscape, half-classical and more than half-Keatsian, that is impossible to locate outside the book's own pages. And yet the preface, written by Phil Stone but presumably approved by Faulkner himself, implicitly invites a localized reading: "The author of these poems is a man steeped in the soil of his native land, a Southerner by every instinct, and, more than that, a Mississippian. George Moore said that all universal art became great by first being provincial, and the sunlight and mocking-birds and blue hills of North Mississippi are a part of this young man's very being."[16]

Faulkner himself might not, even in 1924, have put it quite like that, but it may be well to recall, before dismissing such flourishes out of hand, that Faulkner did subsequently prove himself to be among the greatest nature-writers of the present century—witness the opening chapter of *Light in August,* the wilderness sections of *Go Down, Moses,* and the ecstatic evocation, at once perceptually primitivist and verbally complex, of Ike Snopes's idyll with his beloved cow in *The Hamlet.* (It is, by the way, well worth setting Hardy's description in *Tess of the d'Urbervilles* of the difference in the quality of light at dawn and at dusk alongside Faulkner's densely specific and richly poetic elaboration of a similar perception in that same section of *The Hamlet.*)[17] Insofar, indeed, as the *Marble Faun* preface can be read as a Faulknerian manifesto it is perhaps best seen as a first (and by no means the last) "posed" gesture toward an as yet imperfectly formulated regionalist position and strategy. Within the volume itself—published by a vanity press at someone's else's expense—Faulkner seems less concerned with taking a regional stand than with committing an unmistakably literary act, publicly identifying himself as an artist.

As with Hardy, temporary exile from his native region seems to have been for Faulkner a prerequisite for the development of full regionalist self-consciousness, although in Faulkner's case the processes of developing awareness and consequent action were greatly speeded up. His visits to New York, New Orleans, and Paris in the mid-1920s look, at least in retrospect, like a series of testings of the waters of the literary centers currently most favored by American writers, and the decisions he then made— to avoid the talking-shops and marketplaces of literature, to devote himself absolutely to the art that would thus become his trade, to stay permanently in Mississippi, and to live a certain kind of regionally authenticated life in a certain kind of historically authenticated house—were absolutely crucial to the character, quality, and sheer quantity of his subsequent work.

Faulkner, unlike Hardy, had no need to break free of an initial profession, for he had refused to adopt one, or of a family background, his people having long been influentially established in northern Mississippi. He had to endure (as did Hardy, as do most writers) some local scorn and distrust of his apparent lack of occupation, but he was able in his early thirties to adopt, with unstrenuous deliberation, a mode of life comparable at least in its externals to that of his locally famous great-grandfather, Colonel William Clark Falkner, the "original" of Colonel Sartoris. The straightforwardness of that act of self-determination seems far removed from the angularity of Hardy's class-conscious return to Dorchester in his middle forties as the architect and owner-occupier of a house whose middle-class solidity and red-bricked modernity almost aggressively asserted its difference from the traditional simplicities of the Bockhampton cottage. Whatever other problems Faulkner may have had to contend with, a sense of class or indeed of any other inferiority was not among them—except insofar as he shared in the general southern sense of exclusion from the national mainstream.

Those basic and subsequently unswerving decisions of Faulkner's about his art and his life and the relationship between them gave his career almost from the first a coherence of shape and consistency of direction that Hardy's tended to lack. Faulkner discovered early and never forgot the truth embodied in André Gide's observation as to the artist's need of "a special world of which he alone has the key." [18] He admired Balzac's having created "an intact world of his own," and for all the extraordinary variety of his own novels—each distinct in technique and indeed in most other respects from all of the others—they do establish, in whatever sequence they are read, something of that same sense of imaginative coherence that he himself so much admired in Balzac. Partly, of course, this is an effect established, as in Balzac, by an extensive use of recurrent characters and recurrent settings. In Hardy there are no recurrent characters proper: a name and even a personality may sometimes be reinvoked—that of William Dewy, for example—but I think I am right in saying that no character is actually on stage, so to speak, in more than one novel. Nor is there much reuse of specific settings, despite the attention paid to topographical detail during the later revisions. *The Mayor of Casterbridge* established, once and for all, the centrality to Wessex of Casterbridge itself; Budmouth turns up a few times, sometimes as a setting, sometimes merely as a point of romantic reference; but for the most part topography tends to function in Hardy as a way of establishing the *particularity* of settings and their distinctiveness one from another. In Faulkner the same settings frequently reappear, so that we become aware of them—of the square in Jefferson, the gaol and the courthouse, the Old Frenchman place, and so on—as locations where a series of significant actions have occurred over time, each potentially relevant to all of the others.

This difference may have derived in part from Faulkner's awareness of addressing an urban and predominantly northern audience in whose perception Mississippi was not merely backward and rural (as Dorset was for Hardy's first readers) but primitive and downright hostile, unvisited and unvisitable—an audience, therefore, for whom the significance and potential symbolism of settings had to be established virtually from scratch. Hardy's city-dwelling audience, on the other hand, saw him as recreating the kind of world to which they or their immediate ancestors had until recently belonged, and for which they already nostalgically, if unrealistically, yearned. He also had a wealth of associative allusion on which to draw. His settings often came front-end-loaded, with readily recognizable significances already built in: Casterbridge speaks of Rome in every street and Budmouth can cite King George III as a character reference. Whereas Mississippi and Yoknapatawpha—leaving aside (as they were left) the rapidly displaced and almost unrecorded Indians—could show only a human history that was at one and the same time remarkably short, remarkably violent, and re- markably destructive of the natural environment. The violence occurred chiefly during that Civil War period to which Faulk- ner's fiction so often returns—though his great-grandfather's three trials for murder and his eventual assassination all oc- curred outside the war years, as did innumerable beatings and lynchings of blacks—but the erosion of the environment was continuous, and the melancholy rhythm of Ike McCaslin's suc- cessive returns to the steadily retreating wilderness in *Go Down, Moses* is only one of several features in that novel that make it discussible as a paradigmatic Faulknerian text.

There is often a sense in which the specifically historical ele- ments in Faulkner's work—always allusive, part of the novel's frame rather than central to its action—function largely as a counterweight to or restraint upon an inherent tendency toward romance. It was in some such terms that Faulkner himself once spoke of the role of the outsider, the unimplicated Canadian Shreve McCannon, in relation to the narrative development of *Absalom, Absalom!*: "Shreve was the commentator that held the thing to something of reality. If Quentin had been let alone to tell it, it would have become completely unreal. It had to have a solvent to keep it real, keep it believable, creditable, otherwise it would have vanished into smoke and fury." [19] Not all readers of the novel would see Shreve in quite those terms, of course: it might equally be argued that a historical reference or the pres- ence of an outsider can serve rather to *authenticate* the intrinsi- cally extravagant and implausible, the narrative surrendered to sound and fury from the start. Perhaps—to turn back to Hardy again for a moment—perhaps it is in some such terms that one should regard those shadowy, anonymous scene-setting observers who appear in the early pages of the Wessex novels but promptly and permanently vanish once the narrative is under way: the un- specified furzecutter invoked in the second paragraph of *The Re- turn of the Native,* the putative "casual observer" who witnesses the arrival of Henchard and his family at Weydon Priors, the anonymous ramblers who first view the landscapes of *The Woodlanders* and *Tess of the d'Urbervilles*. It is as if by introducing such unidentified observers Hardy sought to give the regional landscapes and setting of his novels an importance and substance that was independent not only of the characters within the narration but also, to some degree, of the otherwise authoritative voice of the narrator himself.

I have already suggested that public avidity for the reassurances of the actual was soon sufficient to turn Wessex into what might perhaps be called an apparent reality, and in Mississippi now the process of actualizing Yoknapatawpha County is well under way. At one level, of course, this is all good clean fun: the biennial Hardy Conference in Dorchester usually coincides exactly with the annual Faulkner Conference in Oxford, Mississippi, as if there were an open season for regional writers as for deer or grouse, and Hardy seems to have taken some satisfaction in his enhancement of the local tourist industry. But there is also a sense—an altogether more serious sense—in which literary regionalism is forever trying to free itself from the trivialization of "local color" and from the widespread view that regionalism is itself a limiting term. One of the reasons why Faulkner is so little appreciated in Britain, I suspect, is that he is often perceived as writing specifically about a region of which the great British reading public knows almost nothing except that it doesn't want to know anything. Hardy's continuing appeal to the same constituency, on the other hand, is based at least in part upon what might be termed the nationalist aspects of his regionalism—the extent to which the Wessex of his creation has been accepted as representative of Britain as a whole.

Hardy and Faulkner themselves seem never to have doubted that their regions were fundamentally of the mind, and while Hardy never achieved, and never sought, Faulkner's intensive and adhesive intertextuality he seems nevertheless to have been —at least to have become—fully conscious of the literary implications of his acts of world-creation. He liked to think that Egdon

Heath might have been the scene of King Lear's madness (and who is to say that it was not?), and he once declared, apropos of *Under the Greenwood Tree*, that Mellstock, based on his native Stinsford, *was* Stoke Poges, the scene of Gray's meditation in a country churchyard. He seems also to have projected, from the very beginning of his career, a universalizing pastoral function—implicit in their very titles—for novels such as *Under the Greenwood Tree, Far from the Madding Crowd,* and *The Wood-landers.* As for Faulkner, his final choice of *The Hamlet* as the title of one of the finest and most distinctively pastoral of his novels effectually asserted its kinship not only with Gray's hamlet and its rude forefathers, not only with Hardy's Mellstock, but with all the hamlets of literature—with Goldsmith's "Sweet Auburn," Washington Irving's Sleepy Hollow, Sherwood Anderson's Winesburg, and the one that must have been tucked away somewhere in the Forest of Arden. The history of Lake Wobegone had not yet been made a matter of public record.

Regional literature is always didactic—that is perhaps what most clearly distinguishes it from "local color"—and Yoknapatawpha County is at one with Wessex, and with the "Elegy Written in a Country Churchyard," in enforcing a characteristically pastoralist reconsideration of the reader's society and its values through implicit comparisons with other and simpler places and times. But Yoknapatawpha goes much further than Wessex in exploiting its own fictiveness, in asserting those narrative and symbolic freedoms special-worldliness ideally bestows. Where Hardy thought of himself as creating a "partly-real, partly-dream" kingdom, only to find the dream portion progressively overbuilt by speculators of the real, Faulkner invested from the start in solid unreal estate, doubtless suspecting that, as Ishmael in *Moby-Dick* says of Queequeg's native country, "It is not down on any map; true places never are."

NOTES

Faulkner and History

1. Faulkner, *Absalom, Absalom!* (New York: Random House, 1936), 361.

2. *Absalom, Absalom!*, 12.

3. Faulkner, *Essays, Speeches & Public Letters*, ed. James B. Meriwether (New York: Random House, 1965), 15–16.

4. Meriwether, ed., *Essays, Speeches*, 17.

5. *Absalom, Absalom!*, 174, 377.

6. *Absalom, Absalom!*, 383.

7. Scott, *Waverley; or, 'Tis Sixty Years Since* (Edinburgh: Archibald Constable, 1814), 1:9–10.

8. Meriwether, ed., *Essays, Speeches*, 120.

9. Millgate, *Thomas Hardy: His Career As a Novelist* (New York: Random House, 1971), 159.

10. Cowley, *The Faulkner-Cowley File: Letters and Memories, 1944–1962* (New York: Viking Press, 1966), 89.

11. *Absalom, Absalom!*, 378.

12. Meriwether, ed., *Essays, Speeches*, 36.

13. Faulkner, *Lion in the Garden: Interviews with William Faulkner, 1926–1962*, ed. James B. Meriwether and Michael Millgate (New York: Random House, 1968), 128.

14. Frederick L. Gwynn and Joseph L. Blotner, eds., *Faulkner in the University: Class Conferences at the University of Virginia, 1957–1958*, (Charlottesville: University of Virginia Press, 1959), 274.

15. See James B. Meriwether, "Notes on the Textual History of *The Sound and the Fury*," *Papers of the Bibliographical Society of America* 56 (Third Quarter, 1962): 289.

16. Wagner, "Jason Compson: The Demands of Honor," *Sewanee Review* 59 (Autumn 1971): 1–14.

17. Faulkner, *Requiem for a Nun* (New York: Random House, 1951), 92.

18. Gwynn and Blotner, eds., *Faulkner in the University*, 145.

19. Gwynn and Blotner, eds., *Faulkner in the University*, 139.

20. My reference in 1976 was to Polk's 1970 University of South Carolina dissertation on *Requiem for a Nun*, since superseded by his *Faulkner's "Requiem for a Nun": A Critical Study* (Bloomington: Indiana University Press, 1981).

21. Warren, *All the King's Men* (New York: Harcourt, Brace, 1946), 464.

22. Meriwether and Millgate, eds., *Lion in the Garden*, 110.

23. Faulkner, *A Fable* (New York: Random House, 1954), 153–54.

24. *A Fable*, 161.

25. Meriwether and Millgate, eds., *Lion in the Garden*, 280.

William Faulkner: The Shape of a Career

1. Faulkner, *These 13* (New York: Jonathan Cape & Harrison Smith, 1931), 352; see also 358.

2. Meriwether and Millgate, eds., *Lion in the Garden*, 255.

3. Gary Lee Stonum, *Faulkner's Career: An Internal Literary History* (Ithaca: Cornell University Press, 1979), esp. 13–40.

4. Gwynn and Blotner, eds., *Faulkner in the University*, 85.

5. Gwynn and Blotner, eds., *Faulkner in the University*, 251–52.

6. Thomas L. McHaney, *William Faulkner's "The Wild Palms": A Study* (Jackson: University Press of Mississippi, 1975), xiii-xiv.

7. Joseph Blotner, ed., *Selected Letters of William Faulkner* (New York: Random House, 1977), 228.

8. Gwynn and Blotner, eds., *Faulkner in the University*, 90.

9. Faulkner, *Sartoris* (New York: Harcourt, Brace, 1929), 172–73.

10. Meriwether and Millgate, eds., *Lion in the Garden*, 39.

11. Faulkner, *The Reivers* (New York: Random House, 1962), 3.

12. Blotner, ed., *Selected Letters*, 107–9.

13. Blotner, ed., *Selected Letters*, 115; Meriwether and Millgate, eds., *Lion in the Garden*, 40.

14. Doreen Fowler and Ann J. Abadie, eds., *Fifty Years of Yoknapatawpha: Faulkner and Yoknapatawpha, 1979* (Jackson: University Press of Mississippi, 1980), 110–33.

15. Gwynn and Blotner, eds., *Faulkner in the University*, 87.

16. *The Collected Poems of W. B. Yeats* (London: Macmillan, 1955), 104.

17. Gwynn and Blotner, eds., *Faulkner in the University*, 108.

18. Meriwether and Millgate, eds., *Lion in the Garden*, 255.

19. Faulkner, "An Introduction for *The Sound and the Fury*," ed. James B. Meriwether, *Southern Review*, n.s. 8 (October 1972), 708.

20. Faulkner, "Introduction" (*Southern Review*), 709.

21. Faulkner, "Introduction" (*Southern Review*), 709.

22. Faulkner, "An Introduction to *The Sound and the Fury*," ed. James B. Meriwether, *Mississippi Quarterly* 26 (Summer 1973): 414–15.

23. Judith Bryant Wittenberg, *Faulkner: The Transfiguration of Biography* (Lincoln: University of Nebraska Press, 1979).

24. Faulkner, *Go Down, Moses and Other Stories* (New York: Random House, 1942), 30.

"A Cosmos of My Own": The Evolution of Yoknapatawpha

1. Gwynn and Blotner, eds., *Faulkner in the University*, 90.

2. Faulkner, *The Mansion* (New York: Random House, 1959), n.p.

3. James B. Meriwether, "The Beginning of the Snopeses"; Professor Meriwether kindly allowed me to read this unpublished paper. Also relevant is his "Faulkner's Essays on Anderson," in *Faulkner: Fifty Years after "The Marble Faun,"* ed. George H. Wolfe (University: University of Alabama Press, 1976), 159–81.

4. *Sartoris*, n.p.

5. Sherwood Anderson, *Winesburg, Ohio: A Group of Tales of Ohio Small Town Life* (New York: B. W. Huebsch, 1919), n.p.

6. Meriwether, ed., *Essays, Speeches*, 8.

7. Meriwether and Millgate, eds., *Lion in the Garden*, 255.

8. Meriwether, ed., *Essays, Speeches*, 8.

9. See, e.g., Faulkner's *Flags in the Dust*, ed. Douglas Day (New York: Random House, 1973), 87.

10. Meriwether and Millgate, eds., *Lion in the Garden*, 251; see also 217.

11. Quentin's ubiquitousness, first drawn to my attention by James B. Meriwether, has also been commented upon by Estella Schoenberg, *Old Tales and Talking: Quentin Compson in William Faulkner's "Absalom, Absalom!" and Related Works* (Jackson: University Press of Mississippi, 1977), 16–29.

12. *These 13,* 207.

13. Blotner, ed., *Selected Letters,* 34.

14. Joseph Blotner, *Faulkner: A Biography* (New York: Random House, 1974), 596–97; see also James B. Meriwether, "Faulkner's Correspondence with *Scribner's Magazine,*" *Proof* 3 (1973): 257.

15. Blotner, *Faulkner: A Biography,* 684; Meriwether, "Faulkner's Correspondence," 264.

16. Blotner, *Faulkner: A Biography,* 634–35; see also Carvel Collins, "The Pairing of *The Sound and the Fury* and *As I Lay Dying,*" *Princeton University Library Chronicle* 18 (Spring 1957): 123.

17. *These 13,* 356.

18. *Absalom, Absalom!,* 378.

19. "Introduction" (*Southern Review*), 710.

20. James B. Meriwether, quoted in *Approaches to the Study of Twentieth-Century Literature* (East Lansing: Michigan State University, 1961), 43–44.

21. *The Mansion,* n.p.

22. Meriwether and Millgate, eds., *Lion in the Garden,* 255.

23. Meriwether and Millgate, eds., *Lion in the Garden,* 255.

24. Meriwether and Millgate, eds., *Lion in the Garden,* 255.

25. James B. Meriwether, "The Novel Faulkner Never Wrote: His *Golden Book* or *Doomsday Book,*" *American Literature* 42 (March 1970): 93–96; Blotner, *Faulkner: A Biography,* 791.

26. Edgar Lee Masters, *Domesday Book* (New York: Mcmillan, 1920), 3–4.

27. Masters, *Domesday Book,* 3, 21.

28. Meriwether and Millgate, eds., *Lion in the Garden,* 133.

29. Gwynn and Blotner, eds., *Faulkner in the University,* 232.

30. John F. Lynen, *The Pastoral Art of Robert Frost* (New Haven: Yale University Press, 1960).

31. Meriwether and Millgate, eds., *Lion in the Garden,* 233; the penultimate word represents my conjectural—though not unconfident—emendation of the original interview's "Lem."

Faulkner's First Trilogy: Sartoris, Sanctuary, and Requiem for a Nun

1. The manuscript and typescript are both in the Alderman Library of the University of Virginia. See James B. Meriwether, *The Liter-*

ary Career of William Faulkner: A Bibliographical Study (Princeton: Princeton University Library, 1961), 66; Michael Millgate, *The Achievement of William Faulkner* (New York: Random House, 1966), 113–17; and Gerald Langford, *Faulkner's Revision of "Sanctuary": A Collation of the Unrevised Galleys and the Published Book* (Austin: University of Texas Press, 1972). Professor Noel Polk kindly made available to me his transcription of the *Sanctuary* typescript (subsequently the basis of his edition, *Sanctuary: The Original Text* [New York: Random House, 1981]).

2. Meriwether and Millgate, eds., *Lion in the Garden,* 132–33.

3. Carvel Collins, "A Note on *Sanctuary,*" *Harvard Advocate* 135 (November 1951): 16.

4. Blotner, ed., *Selected Letters,* 17.

5. *Sanctuary* typescript, f. 20.

6. *Sartoris,* 302–3.

7. *Sanctuary* typescript, f. 18.

8. *Sanctuary* typescript, f. 321.

9. See Wittenberg, *Faulkner,* 94–95.

10. Albert Devlin, "*Sartoris:* Rereading the MacCallum Episode," *Twentieth Century Literature* 17 (1971): 83–90.

11. Faulkner, *Sanctuary* (New York: Jonathan Cape & Harrison Smith, 1931), 358, 185.

12. *Sanctuary,* 380. The original title of the story, however, appears to have been "Through the Window"; see James B. Meriwether, "The Short Fiction of William Faulkner: A Bibliography," *Proof* 1 (1971): 309.

13. See, for example, the correction to p. 208 of the *Requiem for a Nun* page-proofs at the University of Virginia and the surviving "six years" on p. 88 of the published text.

14. See Noel Polk, "The Textual History of Faulkner's *Requiem for a Nun,*" *Proof* 4 (1975): 113. Professor Polk kindly made available to me his transcription of the manuscript leaves.

15. Blotner, ed., *Selected Letters,* 75.

16. *Sanctuary* typescript, f. 28.

17. Meriwether and Millgate, eds., *Lion in the Garden,* 247.

18. Collins, "Pairing," 114–23; Millgate, *Achievement,* 106.

19. Meriwether and Millgate, eds., *Lion in the Garden,* 239.

20. *Absalom, Absalom!,* 356.

21. Meriwether, ed., *Essays, Speeches,* 120.

22. Blotner, ed., *Selected Letters,* 278.

William Faulkner: The Two Voices

1. Faulkner, *Light in August* (New York: Harrison Smith & Robert Haas, 1932), 301.

2. Walter J. Slatoff, *Quest for Failure: A Study of William Faulkner* (Ithaca: Cornell University Press, 1959), 4.

3. Wittenberg, *Faulkner,* 78, 111.

4. Faulkner, *The Hamlet* (New York: Random House, 1940), 412, 53.

5. Blotner, ed., *Selected Letters,* 142.

6. Polk, *Faulkner's "Requiem for a Nun,"* n.p.

7. Hardy, *Jude the Obscure* (London: Macmillan, 1912), viii.

8. Meriwether, ed., *Essays, Speeches,* 119.

9. Brooks, *William Faulkner: The Yoknapatawpha Country* (New Haven: Yale University Press, 1963), 10–28.

10. Blotner, ed., *Selected Letters,* 215–16.

11. Brooks, *William Faulkner,* 203; see also his "Faulkner and Yeats," in Wolfe, *Fifty Years,* 139–58.

12. Meriwether, ed., *Essays, Speeches,* 146–51.

Faulkner's Masters

1. Adams, "The Apprenticeship of William Faulkner," *Tulane Studies in English* 12 (1962): 113–56; see also his "Faulkner: The European Roots," in Wolfe, *Fifty Years,* 21–41.

2. Adams, "The Apprenticeship," 113–14.

3. Listed by Joseph Blotner in *William Faulkner's Library—A Catalogue* (Charlottesville: University Press of Virginia, 1964).

4. Meriwether and Millgate, eds., *Lion in the Garden,* 110–11.

5. Meriwether and Millgate, eds., *Lion in the Garden,* 17, 21.

6. Meriwether and Millgate, eds., *Lion in the Garden,* 112.

7. Kreiswirth, "Faulkner as Translator: His Versions of Verlaine," *Mississippi Quarterly* 30 (Summer 1977): 429–32.

8. Meriwether and Millgate, eds., *Lion in the Garden,* 128.

9. Meriwether and Millgate, eds., *Lion in the Garden,* 250.

10. Adams, "The Apprenticeship," 139; Blotner, ed., *Selected Letters,* 255–56, 261.

11. Gwynn and Blotner, eds., *Faulkner in the University*, 53.

12. Gwynn and Blotner, eds., *Faulkner in the University*, 280.

13. Meriwether, ed., *Essays, Speeches*, 7.

14. *Flags in the Dust*, 173; the words "O sweety all your little girl-white up I saw" appear near the end of the "Nausicaa" section of *Ulysses*.

15. Gwynn and Blotner, eds., *Faulkner in the University*, 20, 88.

16. A copy of the first edition of 1926, with an undated inscription by Faulkner, is listed by Blotner in *William Faulkner's Library*, 49.

17. Dillon, "Some Sources for Faulkner's Version of the First Air War," *American Literature* 44 (January 1973): 630–32.

18. Blotner, *William Faulkner's Library*, 13.

19. Blotner, ed., *Selected Letters*, 30.

20. Faulkner, "Introduction" (*Southern Review*), 708, 709.

21. Adams, "The Apprenticeship," 129–35.

22. Guerard, *Conrad the Novelist* (Cambridge: Harvard University Press, 1965), 267, 270.

23. Minter, *The Interpreted Design as a Structural Principle in American Prose* (New Haven: Yale University Press, 1969), 8, 191–219.

24. For the use of "inscrutable" by both authors see *Lord Jim: A Tale* (London: William Heinemann, 1921), 517, and *Absalom, Absalom!*, 101. See also Stephen M. Ross, "Conrad's Influence on Faulkner's *Absalom, Absalom!*," *Studies in American Fiction* 2 (Autumn 1974): 199–209, and, for a broader linking of Faulkner with both Conrad and Melville, James Guetti's *The Limits of Metaphor: A Study of Melville, Conrad, and Faulkner* (Ithaca: Cornell University Press, 1967).

25. Meriwether and Millgate, eds., *Lion in the Garden*, 247.

26. For this last point see Laurence Michel, *The Thing Contained: Theory of the Tragic* (Bloomington: Indiana University Press, 1970), 112.

27. Meriwether, ed., *Essays, Speeches*, 197.

28. Gwynn and Blotner, eds., *Faulkner in the University*, 56.

29. Guerard, *The Triumph of the Novel: Dickens, Dostoevsky, Faulkner* (New York: Oxford University Press, 1976).

30. Gwynn and Blotner, eds., *Faulkner in the University*, 56.

31. Meriwether and Millgate, eds., *Lion in the Garden*, 72; see also 217. Faulkner must surely have said "pencil"; his French interviewer may have misheard or been himself mistranslated.

32. Maugham, *Cakes and Ale* (London: William Heinemann, 1930), 118: "[Edward Driffield] was for long thought to write very bad English, and indeed he gave you the impression of writing with the stub of a blunt pencil."

33. Meriwether and Millgate, eds., *Lion in the Garden*, 114–15; Gwynn and Blotner, eds., *Faulkner in the University*, 168–69.

34. Gwynn and Blotner, eds., *Faulkner in the University*, 243.

35. Thackeray, *Vanity Fair: A Novel Without a Hero*, ed. Geoffrey and Kathleen Tillotson (Boston: Houghton Mifflin, 1963), 395.

36. Listed in Blotner, *William Faulkner's Library*, 113.

37. Meriwether and Millgate, eds., *Lion in the Garden*, 128.

Undue Process: Faulkner and the Law

1. Morris Wolff, "Faulkner's Knowledge of the Law," *Mississippi College Law Review* 5 (Spring 1984): 245. See also the articles by Noel Polk and Thomas L. McHaney in the same issue.

2. Published as *Sanctuary: The Original Text.*

3. *Sanctuary*, 135.

4. "Introduction," *Sanctuary* (New York: Modern Library, 1932), v–vi; reprinted in Meriwether, ed., *Essays, Speeches*, 176–78, and *Sanctuary: The Corrected Text*, ed. Noel Polk (New York: Vintage, 1987), 337–39.

5. Henry Seidel Canby, "The School of Cruelty," *Saturday Review of Literature*, 21 March 1931, quoted in John Bassett, ed., *William Faulkner: The Critical Heritage* (London: Routledge & Kegan Paul, 1975), 109.

6. *Sanctuary*, 151.

7. Collins, "A Note on *Sanctuary*," 16.

8. *Sanctuary*, 378.

9. *Sanctuary*, 60.

10. *Sanctuary*, 252.

11. *Sanctuary*, 156.

12. *Sanctuary*, 62.

13. *Sanctuary*, 343.

14. *Sanctuary*, 342, 343.

15. *Sanctuary*, 342, 343, 361, 322.

16. Urgo, "Temple Drake's Truthful Perjury: Rethinking Faulkner's *Sanctuary*," *American Literature* 55 (October 1983): 435–44.

17. *Sanctuary,* 345, 344.

18. *Sanctuary,* 118.

19. See, for example, Urgo, 441–42.

20. *Sanctuary,* 115.

21. *Sanctuary,* 359.

Unreal Estate: Reflections on Wessex and Yoknapatawpha

1. Blotner, *William Faulkner's Library,* 67.

2. Pound, review of Jean Cocteau, *Poesies, 1917–1920,* in *The Dial* 70 (January 1921): 110.

3. Hardy, *The Woodlanders* (London: Macmillan, 1912), 146.

4. Hardy, *The Woodlanders,* 4.

5. *Sunday Times* (London), 24 November 1985, 41.

6. See, for example, K. D. M. Snell, *Annals of the Labouring Poor: Social Change and Agrarian England, 1660–1900* (Cambridge: Cambridge University Press, 1985), 396.

7. Hardy, *The Life and Work of Thomas Hardy,* ed. Michael Millgate (London: Macmillan, 1984), 36.

8. Hardy, *Far from the Madding Crowd* (London: Osgood, McIlvaine, 1895), v.

9. *Thomas Hardy's Personal Writings,* ed. Harold Orel (Lawrence: University Press of Kansas, 1969), 111.

10. Keith, "Thomas Hardy and the Literary Pilgrims," *Nineteenth-Century Fiction,* 24 (June 1969), 80–92.

11. Hardy, *Far from the Madding Crowd,* vi.

12. *Thomas Hardy's Personal Writings,* 46.

13. Meriwether and Millgate, eds., *Lion in the Garden,* 255.

14. Meriwether and Millgate, eds., *Lion in the Garden,* 239.

15. Blotner, ed., *Selected Letters,* 339.

16. Faulkner, *The Marble Faun and A Green Bough* (New York: Random House, 1965), 7.

17. Hardy, *Tess of the d'Urbervilles* (London: Macmillan, 1912), 166; *The Hamlet,* 207.

18. André Gide, *Journals, 1889–1949,* ed. Justin O'Brien (Harmondsworth: Penguin, 1967), 54.

19. Gwynn and Blotner, eds., *Faulkner in the University,* 75.

INDEX

73, 107; author's note to, 25,
47, 56
Marble Faun, The, 7, 19, 73;
preface to, as manifesto,
122–23, 123
Marionettes, 73
Marlowe, Christopher:
Dr. Faustus, 73
Marshal, 13, 72
Masters, Edgar Lee, 49–50
Maugham, Somerset, 93, 136
(n. 32)
McHaney, Thomas L., xii, 72
Melville, Herman, xii, 95, 135
(n. 24); *Moby-Dick*, 61–62, 67,
84, 90, 91–92, 128
Memphis, Tenn., 38, 63–64
Meriwether, James B., xii, 36, 49,
131 (nn. 3, 11)
Mink Snopes, 64, 75, 107
Minter, David L., 90
"Mississippi," 2, 3, 7, 11
Mississippi, 45, 63, 77, 97,
99–100, 106, 122–27 passim
Mississippi, University of, ix, xi
Mitchell, Margaret: *Gone With
the Wind*, 2
Montgomery Ward Snopes, 25
Moore, George, 122–23
Mosquitoes, 25, 53, 63, 73, 86,
87, 120

Nagano seminars, 9, 14, 50,
83–85
Nancy (in "That Evening Sun"),
61
Nancy Mannigoe, 10, 13, 24

Narcissa Benbow, 55–57, 71, 103,
105
Narrative methods, 9–10, 26,
70–73, 79; tall tale, 23, 40–42;
structure, 23, 90, 98–99;
"Gothicism," 91–92
Neil Karens ("Popeye")
Pumphrey, 24, 56, 58, 60, 73,
99, 100–101, 103–5, 108
Nelson, Horatio, 58
New Orleans, La., 38, 63, 87, 120
Nobel Prize address, 4, 75, 76

Old Frenchman place, 58, 65, 74,
102, 104–5, 125
Old Man Gowrie, 74
"Old People, The," 45
Oxford, Miss., 38

Paris Review interview, 18, 29,
36, 38, 39, 47, 48–49, 50
Pastoralism, 51, 76–79, 128
Pat Stamper, 74
Percy Grimm, 72
Polk, Noel, xii, 13, 26, 75, 108,
130 (n. 20), 132 (n. 1), 133
(n. 14)
Popeye, 24, 56, 58, 60, 73, 99,
100–101, 103–5, 108
"Portrait of Elmer Hodge," 86
Pound, Ezra, 112
Proust, Marcel, 19, 84–85, 88
Pylon, 27, 31, 63

Quentin Compson, 1–2, 3,
5, 6–7, 8, 13, 24, 40–45
passim, 64, 71–72; as pivotal

86, 120; social contrasts in, 70–71, 76

Sound and the Fury, The, 21, 22, 26, 28, 33, 38, 56, 63, 68, 73, 76; technique of, 9, 9–10, 44, 71, 88; composition of, 10, 20, 24, 27, 30, 45–46, 54–55; draft introductions to, 29–30, 31–32, 46; and *Absalom, Absalom!,* 44, 45, 62, 64, 65–66; and works by other novelists, 86, 89, 90, 93–94

Southern Historical Association, Faulkner's speech to, 80

"Spotted Horses," 36, 40, 43–44

Stein, Jean. See *Paris Review* interview

Stevenson, Robert Louis: *Treasure Island,* 37

Stone, Phil, 36, 96–97, 103, 122

Stonum, Gary Lee, 18–19

Temple Drake, 10, 13, 59, 103–5, 107–8; and social class, 57, 58, 61, 101

Tennyson, Alfred, 69, 70, 80

Thackeray, William Makepeace, 5, 93; *Vanity Fair,* 93–94

"That Evening Sun," 40, 41, 61, 63

"There Was a Queen," 39, 59, 66, 133 (n. 12)

These 13, 23

Thomas Sutpen, 5, 6, 64, 66, 72

Town, The, 24, 25, 28, 47, 62, 64, 66, 72

Trollope, Anthony, 116

Unvanquished, The, 2, 3, 5, 67; as related to other texts, 23, 24, 25, 63, 66

Urgo, Joseph R., 104–5

Violence, in novels, 99–100, 106, 126

Virginia, University of, xi, 11, 12, 22, 28, 86–87, 91–92, 93

V. K. Suratt, 40, 42. *See also* V. K. Ratliff

Wagner, Linda, 10

Warren, Robert Penn: *All the King's Men,* 14

Wasson, Ben, 10, 53, 54

Wheeler, Daniel Edwin, 94

Whitman, Walt, 16

Wild Palms, The, 20–21, 22, 26, 31, 63, 68; structure of, 72, 73

Will Falls, 43

"With Caution and Dispatch," 24

Wittenberg, Judith, 32, 71

World War I, 3–4, 6, 57

World War II, 21, 59

Yeats, W. B., 28, 78–79

Yoknapatawpha County, xiv, 5, 11, 18, 38, 57, 74, 99–100, 106; evolution of, 22, 23–26, 28, 31, 32, 35–51 passim, 65, 67; topography of, 32, 38; and Thomas Hardy's Wessex, 37–38, 39, 94, 111, 120–26 passim, 127–28; maps of, 38, 45, 46, 47, 76; and Honoré de Balzac, 93